BRITISH HISTORY

Observations & Assessments from Early Cultures to Today

M000106539

TEACHER GUIDE

James P. Stobaugh

1 course = **1** full credit of history

- Includes: Answer Keys
- Student Objectives
- Weekly Tests

First printing: March 2012
Third printing: July 2014

ISBN: 978-0-89051-645-4
ISBN: 978-1-61458-139-0 (ebook)

Cover design by Diana Bogardus.
Interior design by Terry White.

Unless otherwise noted, all images are from shutterstock.com, Library of Congress (LOC-image), and Wikimedia Commons. All images used under the Creative Commons Attribution-Share Alike 3.0 Unported license (CC-BY-SA-3.0) are noted; license details available at creativecommons.org/licenses/by-sa/3.0/.

Scripture quotations taken from The Holy Bible, New International Version®, Copyright © 1973, 1978, 1984, 2011 by Biblica, Inc.™ Used by permission of Zondervan, All rights reserved worldwide.

Please consider requesting that a copy of this volume be purchased by your local library system.

Printed in the United States of America

Please visit our website for other great titles:
www.masterbooks.net

For information regarding author interviews, please contact the publicity department at (870) 438-5288

Master
Books®
A Division of New Leaf Publishing Group
www.masterbooks.net

This book is dedicated to this new generation of young believers whose fervor and dedication to the purposes of the Lord shall yet bring a great revival. Stand tall, young people, and serve our Lord with alacrity and courage!

Since 1975, Master Books has been providing educational resources based on a biblical worldview to students of all ages. At the heart of these resources is our firm belief in a literal six-day creation, a young earth, the global Flood as revealed in Genesis 1–11, and other vital evidence to help build a critical foundation of scriptural authority for everyone. By equipping students with biblical truths and their key connection to the world of science and history, it is our hope they will be able to defend their faith in a skeptical, fallen world.

If the foundations are destroyed, what can the righteous do?
Psalm 11:3; NKJV

As the largest publisher of creation science materials in the world, Master Books is honored to partner with our authors and educators, including:

Ken Ham of Answers in Genesis

Dr. John Morris and Dr. Jason Lisle of the Institute for Creation Research

Dr. Donald DeYoung and Michael Oard of the Creation Research Society

Dr. James Stobaugh, John Hudson Tiner, Rick and Marilyn Boyer, Dr. Tom DeRosa, Todd Friel, Israel Wayne and so many more!

Whether a preschool learner or a scholar seeking an advanced degree, we offer a wonderful selection of award-winning resources for all ages and educational levels.

But sanctify the Lord God in your hearts, and always be ready
to give a defense to everyone who asks you a reason for the hope
that is in you, with meekness and fear.
1 Peter 3:15; NKJV

Permission to Copy

Lessons for a 34-week course!

Overview: This *British History Teacher Guide* contains materials for use with *British History* by James Stobaugh. Materials are organized by book in the following sections:

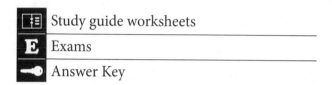

	Study guide worksheets
E	Exams
	Answer Key

Features: Each suggested weekly schedule has five easy-to-manage lessons that combine reading, worksheets, and exams. Worksheets and exams are perforated and three-hole punched – materials are easy to tear out, hand out, grade, and store. You are encouraged to adjust the schedule and materials needed to best work within your educational program.

Workflow: Students will read the pages in their book and then complete each section of the Teacher Guide. Exams are given at regular intervals with space to record each grade. If used with younger students, they may be given the option of taking open-book exams.

Lesson Scheduling: Space is given for assignment dates. There is flexibility in scheduling. For example, the parent may opt for a M, W, F schedule, rather than a M-F schedule. Each week listed has five days but due to vacations the school work week may not be M–F. Adapt the days to your school schedule. As the student completes each assignment, he/she should put an "X" in the box.

🕐	Approximately 20 to 30 minutes per lesson, five days a week
🔑	Includes answer keys for worksheets and exams
📑	Worksheets for each section
🔄	Exams are included to help reinforce learning and provide assessment opportunities
📄	Designed for grades 10 to 12 in a one-year course to earn 1 history credit

Dr. James Stobaugh was a Merrill Fellow at Harvard and holds degrees from Vanderbilt and Rutgers universities, and Princeton and Gordon-Conwell seminaries. An experienced teacher, he is a recognized leader in homeschooling and has published numerous books for students and teachers, including a high school history series (American, British, and World), as well as a companion high school literature series. He and his wife Karen have homeschooled their four children since 1985.

Contents

Introduction

How this course has been developed:

1. **Teacher:** this allows one to study the student objectives with each chapter, providing the answers to the assignments and the weekly exam.

2. **Chapters:** this course has 34 chapters (representing 34 weeks of study).

3. **Lessons:** each chapter has 5 lessons each, taking approximately 20 to 30 minutes each. There will be a short reading followed by critical thinking questions. Some questions require a specific answer from the text where others are more open-ended, leading the student to think "outside the box."

4. **Weekly exams:** the final lesson of the week is the exam covering the week's chapter. Students are not to use their text to answer these questions unless otherwise directed.

5. **Student responsibility:** Responsibility to complete this course is on the student. Students are to complete the readings every day, handing their responses to a parent or teacher for evaluation. Independence is strongly encouraged in this course designed for the student to practice independent learning.

6. **Grading:** A parent or teacher can grade assignments daily or weekly, and keep track of this in their files. Assignments with answers are available at the end of each chapter.

First Semester Suggested Daily Schedule

Date	Day	Assignment	Due Date	✓	Grade
		First Semester — First Quarter			
Week 1	Day 1	**Chapter 1: Early England: Part One** Read **Lesson 1 — The Beginning** Student Book (SB) Complete Assignment Page 19 Lesson Planner (TG)			
	Day 2	Read **Lesson 2 — Picts, Scots, Britons, and Angles** (SB) Complete Assignment Page 20 (TG)			
	Day 3	Read **Lesson 3 — Druids** (SB) Complete Assignment Page 21 (TG)			
	Day 4	Read **Lesson 4 — Ancient British Life** (SB) Complete Assignment Page 22 (TG)			
	Day 5	**Chapter 1 Exam** Pages 157–158 (TG)			
Week 2	Day 6	**Chapter 2: Early England: Part Two** Read **Lesson 1 — Roman England** (SB) Complete Assignment Page 23 (TG)			
	Day 7	Read **Lesson 2 — The Legend of King Arthur** (SB) Complete Assignment Page 24 (TG)			
	Day 8	Read **Lesson 3 — King Arthur** (SB) Complete Assignment Page 25 (TG)			
	Day 9	Read **Lesson 4 — An Early Roman City: London** (SB) Complete Assignment Page 26 (TG)			
	Day 10	**Chapter 2 Exam** Pages 159–160 (TG)			
Week 3	Day 11	**Chapter 3: Anglo-Saxon Invasions** Read **Lesson 1 — Anglo-Saxon Invasions** (SB) Complete Assignment Page 27 (TG)			
	Day 12	Read **Lesson 2 — Christianity in England** (SB) Complete Assignment Page 28 (TG)			
	Day 13	Read **Lesson 3 — Anglo-Saxon London** (SB) Complete Assignment Page 29 (TG)			
	Day 14	Read **Lesson 4 — Viking Invasions of England** (SB) Complete Assignment Page 30 (TG)			
	Day 15	**Chapter 3 Exam** Pages 161–162 (TG)			
Week 4	Day 16	**Chapter 4: The Norman Conquest** Read **Lesson 1 — Norman Conquest** (SB) Complete Assignment Page 31 (TG)			
	Day 17	Read **Lesson 2 — The Plantagenets** (SB) Complete Assignment Page 32 (TG)			
	Day 18	Read **Lesson 3 — London: 1166–1550** (SB) Complete Assignment Page 33 (TG)			
	Day 19	Read **Lesson 4 — Philosophers and World Views** (SB) Complete Assignment Page 34 (TG)			
	Day 20	**Chapter 4 Exam** Pages 163–164 (TG)			

Date	Day	Assignment	Due Date	✓	Grade
Week 5	Day 21	**Chapter 5: Henry VIII and the English Reformation** Read **Lesson 1 — Henry VIII** (SB) Complete Assignment Page 35 (TG)			
	Day 22	Read **Lesson 2 — The English Reformation** (SB) Complete Assignment Page 36 (TG)			
	Day 23	Read **Lesson 3 — London** (SB) Complete Assignment Page 37 (TG)			
	Day 24	Read **Lesson 4 — History Maker: Sir Thomas More** (SB) Complete Assignment Page 38 (TG)			
	Day 25	**Chapter 5 Exam** Pages 165–166 (TG)			
Week 6	Day 26	**Chapter 6: Elizabethan Age: Part One** Read **Lesson 1 — Elizabethan Age** (SB) Complete Assignment Page 39 (TG)			
	Day 27	Read **Lesson 2 — The Spanish Armada** (SB) Complete Assignment Page 40 (TG)			
	Day 28	Read **Lesson 3 — English Age of Exploration** (SB) Complete Assignment Page 41 (TG)			
	Day 29	Read **Lesson 4 — Elizabethan London** (SB) Complete Assignment Page 42 (TG)			
	Day 30	**Chapter 6 Exam** Pages 167–168 (TG)			
Week 7	Day 31	**Chapter 7: Elizabethan Age: Part Two** Read **Lesson 1 — Elizabethan Life** (SB) Complete Assignment Page 43 (TG)			
	Day 32	Read **Lesson 2 — Scotland in the Elizabethan Age** (SB) Complete Assignment Page 44 (TG)			
	Day 33	Read **Lesson 3 — Philosophers and World Views** (SB) Complete Assignment Page 45 (TG)			
	Day 34	Read **Lesson 4 — The Evolution of Parliament** (SB) Complete Assignment Page 46 (TG)			
	Day 35	**Chapter 7 Exam** Page 169 (TG)			
Week 8	Day 36	**Chapter 8: The Golden Age** Read **Lesson 1 — Elizabethan Social Welfare** (SB) Complete Assignment Page 47 (TG)			
	Day 37	Read **Lesson 2 — Superstition and Witchcraft** (SB) Complete Assignment Page 48 (TG)			
	Day 38	Read **Lesson 3 — Medicine** (SB) Complete Assignment Page 49 (TG)			
	Day 39	Read **Lesson 4 — Literature and Art** (SB) Complete Assignment Page 50 (TG)			
	Day 40	**Chapter 8 Exam** Pages 171–172 (TG)			

Date	Day	Assignment	Due Date	✓	Grade
Week 9	Day 41	**Chapter 9: The Early Stuarts** Read **Lesson 1 — The Early Stuarts** (SB) Complete Assignment Page 51 (TG)			
	Day 42	Read **Lesson 2 — The Gunpowder Plot** (SB) Complete Assignment Page 52 (TG)			
	Day 43	Read **Lesson 3 — Stuart London** (SB) Complete Assignment Page 53 (TG)			
	Day 44	Read **Lesson 4 — The King James Bible** (SB) Complete Assignment Page 54 (TG)			
	Day 45	**Chapter 9 Exam** Page 173 (TG)			
First Semester — Second Quarter					
Week 1	Day 46	**Chapter 10: The English Civil War** Read **Lesson 1 — Charles I** (SB) Complete Assignment Page 55 (TG)			
	Day 47	Read **Lesson 2 — The English Civil War** (SB) Complete Assignment Page 56 (TG)			
	Day 48	Read **Lesson 3 — Puritanism** (SB) Complete Assignment Page 57 (TG)			
	Day 49	Read **Lesson 4 — Oliver Cromwell** (SB) Complete Assignment Page 58 (TG)			
	Day 50	**Chapter 10 Exam** Pages 175–176 (TG)			
Week 2	Day 51	**Chapter 11: The Commonwealth** Read **Lesson 1 — Historical Debate: English Civil War** (SB) Complete Assignment Page 59 (TG)			
	Day 52	Read **Lesson 2 — The Commonwealth** (SB) Complete Assignment Page 60 (TG)			
	Day 53	Read **Lesson 3 — The Early British Empire** (SB) Complete Assignment Page 61 (TG)			
	Day 54	Read **Lesson 4 — The East India Company** (SB) Complete Assignment Page 62 (TG)			
	Day 55	**Chapter 11 Exam** Pages 177–178 (TG)			
Week 3	Day 56	**Chapter 12: The Restoration** Read **Lesson 1 — The Restoration** (SB) Complete Assignment Page 63 (TG)			
	Day 57	Read **Lesson 2 — Great Fire of London** (SB) Complete Assignment Page 64 (TG)			
	Day 58	Read **Lesson 3 — The History of Ireland** (SB) Complete Assignment Page 65 (TG)			
	Day 59	Read **Lesson 4 — Philosophers and World Views** (SB) Complete Assignment Page 66 (TG)			
	Day 60	**Chapter 12 Exam** Pages 179–180 (TG)			

Date	Day	Assignment	Due Date	✓	Grade
Week 4	Day 61	**Chapter 13: The Glorious Revolution** Read **Lesson 1 — The Glorious Revolution** (SB) Complete Assignment Page 67 (TG)			
	Day 62	Read **Lesson 2 — The Declaration of Right; February 13, 1689** (SB) Complete Assignment Page 68 (TG)			
	Day 63	Read **Lesson 3 — Women During the Glorious Revolution** (SB) Complete Assignment Page 69 (TG)			
	Day 64	Read **Lesson 4 — Historical Debate** (SB) Complete Assignment Page 70 (TG)			
	Day 65	**Chapter 13 Exam** Page 181 (TG)			
Week 5	Day 66	**Chapter 14: The Oranges, Stuarts, and Hanovers** Read **Lesson 1 — The Reign of William and Mary** (SB) Complete Assignment Page 71 (TG)			
	Day 67	Read **Lesson 2 — Queen Anne** (SB) Complete Assignment Page 72 (TG)			
	Day 68	Read **Lesson 3 — George I** (SB) Complete Assignment Page 73 (TG)			
	Day 69	Read **Lesson 4 — William Penn** (SB) Complete Assignment Page 74 (TG)			
	Day 70	**Chapter 14 Exam** Pages 183–184 (TG)			
Week 6	Day 71	**Chapter 15: Whigs and Tories** Read **Lesson 1 — Whigs and Tories** (SB) Complete Assignment Page 75 (TG)			
	Day 72	Read **Lesson 2 — George II** (SB) Complete Assignment Page 76 (TG)			
	Day 73	Read **Lesson 3 — George III** (SB) Complete Assignment Page 77 (TG)			
	Day 74	Read **Lesson 4 — Georgian London** (SB) Complete Assignment Page 78 (TG)			
	Day 75	**Chapter 15 Exam** Pages 185–186 (TG)			
Week 7	Day 76	**Chapter 16: European Wars** Read **Lesson 1 — King William's War** (SB) Complete Assignment Page 79 (TG)			
	Day 77	Read **Lesson 2 — War of the Spanish Succession** (SB) Complete Assignment Page 80 (TG)			
	Day 78	Read **Lesson 3 — War of the Austrian Succession** (SB) Complete Assignment Page 81 (TG)			
	Day 79	Read **Lesson 4 — Seven Year's War** (SB) Complete Assignment Page 82 (TG)			
	Day 80	**Chapter 16 Exam** Pages 187–188 (TG)			

Date	Day	Assignment	Due Date	✓	Grade
Week 8	Day 81	**Chapter 17: British Empire** Read **Lesson 1 — Empire** (SB) Complete Assignment Page 83 (TG)			
	Day 82	Read **Lesson 2 — Mercantilism** (SB) Complete Assignment Page 84 (TG)			
	Day 83	Read **Lesson 3 — English Rule in India** (SB) Complete Assignment Page 85 (TG)			
	Day 84	Read **Lesson 4 — The American Revolution** (SB) Complete Assignment Page 86 (TG)			
	Day 85	**Chapter 17 Exam** Pages 189–190 (TG)			
Week 9	Day 86	**Chapter 18: Response to the French Revolution** Read **Lesson 1 — Response to the French Revolution** (SB) Complete Assignment Page 87 (TG)			
	Day 87	Read **Lesson 2 — The Revolution Controversy** (SB) Complete Assignment Page 88 (TG)			
	Day 88	Read **Lesson 3 — Primary Sources** (SB) Complete Assignment Page 89 (TG)			
	Day 89	Read **Lesson 4 — An Early History** (SB) Complete Assignment Page 90 (TG)			
	Day 90	**Chapter 18 Exam** Pages 191–192 (TG)			
		Midterm Grade			

Date	Day	Assignment	Due Date	✓	Grade
Week 1	Day 91	**Chapter 19: Philosophers and World Views** Read **Lesson 1 — William Godwin** (SB) Complete Assignment Page 91 (TG)			
	Day 92	Read **Lesson 2 — Jean-Jacques Rousseau** (SB) Complete Assignment Page 92 (TG)			
	Day 93	Read **Lesson 3 — Edmund Burke** (SB) Complete Assignment Page 93 (TG)			
	Day 94	Read **Lesson 4 — Thomas Paine** (SB) Complete Assignment Page 94 (TG)			
	Day 95	**Chapter 19 Exam** Page 193 (TG)			
Week 2	Day 96	**Chapter 20: The Age of Napoleon** Read **Lesson 1 — The Age of Napoleon: Part One** (SB) Complete Assignment Page 95 (TG)			
	Day 97	Read **Lesson 2 — The Age of Napoleon: Part Two** (SB) Complete Assignment Page 96 (TG)			
	Day 98	Read **Lesson 3 — The Age of Napoleon: Part Three** (SB) Complete Assignment Page 97 (TG)			
	Day 99	Read **Lesson 4 — The Napoleon of the People** (SB) Complete Assignment Page 98 (TG)			
	Day 100	**Chapter 20 Exam** Page 195 (TG)			
Week 3	Day 101	**Chapter 21: The Industrial Revolution** Read **Lesson 1 — The Industrial Revolution** (SB) Complete Assignment Page 99 (TG)			
	Day 102	Read **Lesson 2 — The Rise of Cities** (SB) Complete Assignment Page 100 (TG)			
	Day 103	Read **Lesson 3 — William Wilberforce** (SB) Complete Assignment Page 101 (TG)			
	Day 104	Read **Lesson 4 — 19th-Century London** (SB) Complete Assignment Page 102 (TG)			
	Day 105	**Chapter 21 Exam** Page 197 (TG)			
Week 4	Day 106	**Chapter 22: 19th-Century England** Read **Lesson 1 — King George IV** (SB) Complete Assignment Page 103 (TG)			
	Day 107	Read **Lesson 2 — William IV** (SB) Complete Assignment Page 104 (TG)			
	Day 108	Read **Lesson 3 — 19th Century English History** (SB) Complete Assignment Page 105 (TG)			
	Day 109	Read **Lesson 4 — The Irish Potato Famine** (SB) Complete Assignment Page 106 (TG)			
	Day 110	**Chapter 22 Exam** Pages 199–200 (TG)			

Second Semester Suggested Daily Schedule

Date	Day	Assignment	Due Date	✓	Grade
Week 5	Day 111	**Chapter 23: Victorian Age** Read **Lesson 1 — The Victorian Age** (SB) Complete Assignment Page 107 (TG)			
	Day 112	Read **Lesson 2 — Emmeline Pankhurst** (SB) Complete Assignment Page 108 (TG)			
	Day 113	Read **Lesson 3 — Philosophers and World Views** (SB) Complete Assignment Page 109 (TG)			
	Day 114	Read **Lesson 4 — Philosophers and World Views** (SB) Complete Assignment Page 110 (TG)			
	Day 115	**Chapter 23 Exam** Page 201 (TG)			
Week 6	Day 116	**Chapter 24: Victorian Life** Read **Lesson 1 — The Decline of Religion** (SB) Complete Assignment Page 111 (TG)			
	Day 117	Read **Lesson 2 — Charles Darwin** (SB) Complete Assignment Page 112 (TG)			
	Day 118	Read **Lesson 3 — William Booth** (SB) Complete Assignment Page 113 (TG)			
	Day 119	Read **Lesson 4 — Florence Nightingale** (SB) Complete Assignment Page 114 (TG)			
	Day 120	**Chapter 24 Exam** Pages 203–204 (TG)			
Week 7	Day 121	**Chapter 25: 19th Century Wars** Read **Lesson 1 — The Afghan Wars** (SB) Complete Assignment Page 115 (TG)			
	Day 122	Read **Lesson 2 — The Crimean War** (SB) Complete Assignment Page 116 (TG)			
	Day 123	Read **Lesson 3 — The Raj Wars** (SB) Complete Assignment Page 117 (TG)			
	Day 124	Read **Lesson 4 — The Second Afghan War** (SB) Complete Assignment Page 118 (TG)			
	Day 125	**Chapter 25 Exam** Pages 205–206 (TG)			
Week 8	Day 126	**Chapter 26: British Colonialism in Africa** Read **Lesson 1 — West Africa** (SB) Complete Assignment Page 119 (TG)			
	Day 127	Read **Lesson 2 — David Livingston** (SB) Complete Assignment Page 120 (TG)			
	Day 128	Read **Lesson 3 — Anglo-Zulu Wars** (SB) Complete Assignment Page 121 (TG)			
	Day 129	Read **Lesson 4 — The Mahdi and the British** (SB) Complete Assignment Page 122 (TG)			
	Day 130	**Chapter 26 Exam** Pages 207–208 (TG)			

Date	Day	Assignment	Due Date	✓	Grade
Week 9	Day 131	**Chapter 27: The New Century** Read **Lesson 1 — The Boer Wars** (SB) Complete Assignment Page 123 (TG)			
	Day 132	Read **Lesson 2 — The Boxer Rebellion** (SB) Complete Assignment Page 124 (TG)			
	Day 133	Read **Lesson 3 — George V** (SB) Complete Assignment Page 125 (TG)			
	Day 134	Read **Lesson 4 — London: Early 20th Century** (SB) Complete Assignment Page 126 (TG)			
	Day 135	**Chapter 27 Exam** Page 209 (TG)			
Second Semester — Fourth Quarter					
Week 1	Day 136	**Chapter 28: Modernism** Read **Lesson 1 — Historical Debate** (SB) Complete Assignment Page 127 (TG)			
	Day 137	Read **Lesson 2 — Modernism** (SB) Complete Assignment Page 128 (TG)			
	Day 138	Read **Lesson 3 — World View and Philosophers** (SB) Complete Assignment Page 129 (TG)			
	Day 139	Read **Lesson 4 — Frankenstein** (SB) Complete Assignment Page 130 (TG)			
	Day 140	**Chapter 28 Exam** Page 211 (TG)			
Week 2	Day 141	**Chapter 29: Causes of World War I** Read **Lesson 1 — Nationalism vs Monarchy** (SB) Complete Assignment Page 131 (TG)			
	Day 142	Read **Lesson 2 — Alliances** (SB) Complete Assignment Page 132 (TG)			
	Day 143	Read **Lesson 3 — The Arms Race** (SB) Complete Assignment Page 133 (TG)			
	Day 144	Read **Lesson 4 — The First Shots** (SB) Complete Assignment Page 134 (TG)			
	Day 145	**Chapter 29 Exam** Pages 213–214 (TG)			
Week 3	Day 146	**Chapter 30: World War I** Read **Lesson 1 — World War I** (SB) Complete Assignment Page 135 (TG)			
	Day 147	Read **Lesson 2 — The Battle of the Somme** (SB) Complete Assignment Page 136 (TG)			
	Day 148	Read **Lesson 3 — The Royal Flying Corps** (SB) Complete Assignment Page 137 (TG)			
	Day 149	Read **Lesson 4 — Winston Churchill** (SB) Complete Assignment Page 138 (TG)			
	Day 150	**Chapter 30 Exam** Page 215 (TG)			

Date	Day	Assignment	Due Date	✓	Grade
Week 4	Day 151	**Chapter 31: World War I and Afterwards** Read **Lesson 1 — Versailles Treaty** (SB) Complete Assignment Page 139 (TG)			
	Day 152	Read **Lesson 2 — Contemporary Voices** (SB) Complete Assignment Page 140 (TG)			
	Day 153	Read **Lesson 3 — The Great Flu Pandemic** (SB) Complete Assignment Page 141 (TG)			
	Day 154	Read **Lesson 4 — Post-War London** (SB) Complete Assignment Page 142 (TG)			
	Day 155	**Chapter 31 Exam** Page 217 (TG)			
Week 5	Day 156	**Chapter 32: Totalitarianism** Read **Lesson 1 — England on the Brink** (SB) Complete Assignment Page 143 (TG)			
	Day 157	Read **Lesson 2 — Totalitarianism: Italy** (SB) Complete Assignment Page 144 (TG)			
	Day 158	Read **Lesson 3 — English Views of Hitler and Stalin** (SB) Complete Assignment Page 145 (TG)			
	Day 159	Read **Lesson 4 — Japan: A More Serious Threat** (SB) Complete Assignment Page 146 (TG)			
	Day 160	**Chapter 32 Exam** Page 219 (TG)			
Week 6	Day 161	**Chapter 33: World War II and the Cold War** Read **Lesson 1 — The Great Slump** (SB) Complete Assignment Page 147 (TG)			
	Day 162	Read **Lesson 2 — Queen Elizabeth II** (SB) Complete Assignment Page 148 (TG)			
	Day 163	Read **Lesson 3 — Appeasement** (SB) Complete Assignment Page 149 (TG)			
	Day 164	Read **Lesson 4 — World War II** (SB) Complete Assignment Page 150 (TG)			
	Day 165	**Chapter 33 Exam** Page 221 (TG)			
Week 7	Day 166	**Chapter 34: The End of an Empire** Read **Lesson 1 — A New Enemy** (SB) Complete Assignment Page 151 (TG)			
	Day 167	Read **Lesson 2 — The Cold War** (SB) Complete Assignment Page 152 (TG)			
	Day 168	Read **Lesson 3 — Historical Essay** (SB) Complete Assignment Page 153 (TG)			
	Day 169	Read **Lesson 4 — 1970s to the Present** (SB) Complete Assignment Page 154 (TG)			
	Day 170	**Chapter 34 Exam** Page 223 (TG)			
		Semester Grade			

Daily Worksheets

Assignment

Why did the early Britons never develop writing?

Assignment

Describe the different tribal groups that settled in Great Britain.

Assignment

A. What role did druids assume in ancient British society?

B. Why is Halloween a dangerous, anti-Christian holiday?

Assignment

Describe a typical Briton family.

Assignment

Imagine that you were a Roman soldier stationed at Hadrian's Wall. What sort of concerns would you have?

Assignment

An epic hero is an important figure from a history or legend who illustrates traits, performs deeds, and exemplifies certain morals that are valued by the society from which the epic originates. Is King Arthur an epic hero? What does the King Arthur legend tell us about English Briton Society?

Assignment

Around the middle of the A.D. 500s, waves of invaders—Jutes and Angles from what is now Denmark and Saxons from northern Germany—commonly known as Anglo-Saxons, invaded England. They settled on the eastern shore near London. They moved westward up the Thames River, looking for more land to cultivate, taking fertile river valleys and leaving hill country to the Celtic Britons. There were some victories against the dreaded Anglo-Saxons. One set of victories occurred through the leadership of Celtic Britain King Arthur. A British monk described Arthur as an emperor from a place called Camelot, and he would write of Arthur defeating the Irish and the Scots, conquering Norway and Denmark, marrying a noble woman named Guinevere and then conquering France. How true are these stories?

Assignment

Rome was faced with major problems both in governing its empire and maintaining peace and security within it. In order to achieve these aims, Rome relied heavily upon her cities. Cities were the primary level of the administration of the empire. It was also the cultural center of the empire. Yet, in a country as rural as England, problems often arose. Speculate upon what some of these problems were and how Rome may have solved them.

Assignment

A. The Anglo-Saxons were a relatively small group of in-vaders, yet, they were able to conquer England. How?

B. What is the difference between Celtic Christianity and Roman Christianity?

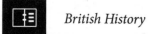
Assignment

Why was the Anglo-Saxon Church so important to the political Anglo-Saxon state?

Assignment

A. Why did the Church choose to locate its headquarters in Canterbury instead of London?

B. Why is King Alfred so important to English history?

Assignment

Why were the Vikings so successful in their initial subjugation of cultures in Northern Europe? They were marginally successful in England. Why did they ultimately fail to have a lasting cultural impact?

Assignment

What impact did the Norman Conquest have on English history?

Assignment

Edward I experienced significant military successes because he implemented the latest technological advances in military hardware—in particular he introduced the Welsh longbow into his army's arsenal. This was a vastly superior implement of war and guaranteed him military success over all his enemies for a generation. Discuss how military advances have benefitted modern states. This question may require some research.

Assignment

Why did London experience unprecedented prosperity during the Norman reign?

Assignment

A. The Scholastics tried to argue from rationalism that God exists and that He is omnipotent. Why is this so difficult?

B. Erasmus suggested something that was innocuous enough: that people should primarily be concerned with their happiness. Why is this a dangerous notion?

C. What does Bacon mean when he implies that scientific knowledge may lead to salvation, but the prerequisite for this revealed wisdom of science is Christian morality? Why is this a dangerous thought?

D. Believing that contradictions were fundamental in the study of logic, to sharpen the minds of his students Abelard found contrary positions. For instance, Abelard challenged his students with this question, "Why does an omnipotent God allow bad things to happen to good people?" Answer Abelard's question.

Assignment

Why was Henry VIII such an important king?

Assignment

An historian argued that, even by the end of the 16th Century, prolonged clerical efforts had succeeded in creating a Protestant nation, but not a nation of Protestants. What did he mean and do you agree?

Assignment

The weakened Church structure had an adverse effect on urban life. Its absence presaged further troubles in London. Church influence in many modern cities has declined in the last 50 years. Discuss how this has had an adverse effect on the city.

Assignment

More fervently opposed the separation of church and state. He strongly believed that the church was the conscience of the state. More said, "I think that when statesmen forsake their own private conscience for the sake of their public duties, they lead their country by a short route to chaos." Do you agree? Why or why not?

Assignment

A. Queen Elizabeth I is considered one of the country's most successful and popular monarchs. But what was Elizabeth really like? Was she wicked? Ambitious? Was her success due to her own skill—or was she a people pleaser?

B. In 1558 John Knox wrote, "It is more than a monster in nature that a woman should reign and bear empire over man." Are women fit to rule kingdoms?

Assignment

Why was the Spanish Armada defeated?

Assignment

Why did the English enter the Age of Exploration relatively late, but, in the long run, explored and owned more land than any other European power?

Assignment

Pretend that you were a regular Globe Theatre patron. What was it like?

Assignment

Contrast your life with the life of an Elizabethan.

Assignment

A. How did Protestant Scotland get connected to Catholic France?

B. John Knox is an enigmatic figure. Do you object to your church leaders carrying weapons and killing the perceived enemies of Christ?

Assignment

A. Why is Hobbes so popular among Marxist historians?

B. The Christian understanding of redemption is an event that occurs outside human experience. As Oswald Chambers explains, "The redemption of Christ is not an experience, it is the great act of God which He has performed through Christ." Given this fact, why are the writings of Descartes so dangerous?

Assignment

Summarize how Parliament evolved into the democratic institution it became.

Assignment

Compare the Elizabethan social welfare system to the present United States social welfare system. Which system is more effective?

Assignment

On July 26, 1566, Joan Waterhouse, 18 years old, called the devil from out of her mother's shoes, expecting a toad. Instead, a great dog came to her, demanding what she would like. She asked him to haunt Agnes Brown, 12, who hadn't given her enough bread once. Agnes Brown said that a thing came to her like a black dog with a face like an ape, a short tail, a chain and a silver whistle around its neck and horns on its head. (From *The Examination and Confession of Certaine Wytches at Chensford* (Chelmsford), 1566). Joan was acquitted.

Agnes Waterhouse of Hatfield Peverell, Essex, known as "Mother Waterhouse," was accused of witchcraft in 1566, along with her daughter, Joan, and Elizabeth Francis. She was said to have bewitched one William Fynne, who had died on November 1565. In a confession, she claimed she had been a witch for 15 years and admitted to killing livestock, bewitching her husband, and trying to kill another man. She said she had tried to use Mrs. Francis's familiar, the cat named Satan, to help her, but that Satan had turned himself into a toad. She denied she had ever succeeded in killing anyone by witchcraft, but she was found guilty of Fynne's death at the Chelmsford assizes and hanged.

Why was one woman acquitted and the other one hanged? Were there really witches? If so, were they punished appropriately?

Assignment

Queen Elizabeth, at one time, tried to institute a sort of "national health program" by enabling her subjects to receive the medical care they needed. It never worked. Why is free national health coverage so hard to offer today?

Assignment

Why did the arts flourish in Elizabethan England?

Assignment

In spite of his best efforts, why was the reign of King James basically ineffectual?

Assignment

Assuming the Gunpowder Plot worked, would it really have made a difference?

Assignment

Describe life in Stuart London.

Assignment

In light of the fact that there were many extant copies of the Bible already (e.g., Geneva Bible), why did King James I feel compelled to authorize another translation?

Assignment

A. This era has also been called the Puritan Revolution because the religious complexion of the king's opponents was overwhelmingly Puritan, and because the defeat of the king was accompanied by the abolition of episcopacy. That argument, however, overemphasizes the religious element at the expense of the constitutional issues and the underlying social and economic factors. What were some of these?

B. Most historians blame Charles I for the English Civil War. When Charles Stuart was a young child, it seemed unlikely that he would survive, let alone become ruler of England and Scotland. Once shy and retiring, an awkward stutterer, he grew in stature and confidence. By all accounts he was a sincere, friendly, yet shy man who was not motivated by base motives. Discuss the causes of the English Civil War from his perspective.

Assignment

A. Why did the Roundheads eventually win the English Civil War?

B. In the final analysis, who was right—the Parliament-arians or the Loyalists? Which side would you join?

Assignment

Historian Perry Miller argued that Puritanism was an intellectual/religious movement whose impact could not be understood without understanding Puritan theology and world view. Later historians criticized Miller for over-intellectualizing Puritanism. They argued that motivation is better connected to social and political forces. In other words, the Puritans were motivated by their social agendas, not by their faith. What do you think?

Assignment

Cromwell brought a king to the scaffold. He executed thousands of Irish and Scottish rebels, all in the name of God. His last prayer was, "Thou hast made me, though very unworthy, a mean instrument to do Thy people some good service . . . " But, did Cromwell go too far? What happens when well-intentioned Christians, even with a pure heart, overcome violence with violence?

Assignment

What caused the English Civil War?

Assignment

Why did the Commonwealth abandon its egalitarian agenda and become an autocracy?

Assignment

In the midst of significant domestic turmoil, the English government was still able to support overseas expansion and colonization. How?

Assignment

Why was the East India Company so successful?

Assignment

Most historians today see Charles II in a very unsympathetic light. They are convinced that Charles was a spoiled, self-centered, indulgent monarch who cared for no one but himself. In *The Last Rally*, 19th century historian Hilaire Belloc disagreed. Restored to the throne following the interlude of Cromwell's Commonwealth, Charles II devoted his life as King of England to maintaining the integrity of the throne against all the forces arrayed against it. The story that Belloc brings to life is thus one of survival: the story of a ship of state brought "through peril and storm under a great captain." Which interpretation is correct?

Assignment

Why was the Great London Fire of 1666 a mixed blessing?

Assignment

Why did the English continue to dominate Irish politics until the 20th century?

Assignment

A. Christians can readily agree with Spinoza, and disagree with him, at the same time. How?

B. On one level Christians agree with Locke (like Spinoza). On another level Christians have to reject Locke's thoughts. Explain.

Assignment

Many historians argue that only in a constitutional monarchy could a bloodless, "glorious" revolution occur. Agree or disagree.

Assignment

Compare and contrast the American Bill of Rights with the English Declaration of Rights.

Assignment

What concerns do these women have and what solutions are they suggesting?

Assignment

Which argument do you find most persuasive? Why?

Assignment

The reign of Mary II and William III marked the end of royal prerogative. Parliament, with the authority of the oligarchy, came into a position of prominence regarding the governing of England. One contemporary described Queen Mary, "She seems to be of a good nature, and that she takes nothing to heart; whilst the Prince her husband has a thoughtful countenance, is wonderfully serious and silent, and seems to treat all persons alike gravely, and to be very intent on affairs: Holland, Ireland, and France calling for his care." In other words, the best thing that can be said of William and Mary is that they did virtually nothing. Was that a good thing for England at the end of the 17th century?

Assignment

Most historians presented Anne as weak, indecisive monarch. The historian Gregg sees Queen Anne as more important and attempts to give a balanced portrayal of her public and private life. Gregg believes that Queen Anne was a strong, careful and calculating monarch, was driven by ambition and resolve, and who asserted her authority without trampling on parliamentary authority. He also portrays Anne pursuing a course of political moderation. She is not someone dominated by changes in the strengths of different political parties. Rather, a monarch not controlled by either party who had ministers from both parties and changed them in order to pursue policies of which she approved. What do you think?

Assignment

How did George I's love for his homeland change English history?

Assignment

Why was William Penn such an effective champion of liberty?

Assignment

Which political position do you find most appealing, Whig or Tory?

Assignment

Many historians argue that Caroline was vital to George II's reign. In fact, they argue, he could not have survived as a sovereign without her. Discuss how Caroline helped her husband become more effective.

Assignment

Rejecting high society in London and the lavish luxuries of court life, King George and his consort Queen Charlotte (1744-1818) preferred to live away from London in what Charlotte referred to as their "sweet retreat," allowing them to focus on family and domestic life. This practice helped to revive the reputation and popularity of the monarchy and marked the beginning of the transition to the modern form of the British court. George was the punctual, abstemious, hard working German. At the same time, George III was going mad. Pretend that you are a member of Parliament in 1800. George III is showing signs of dementia. At what point do you replace him? What dangers would you encounter if you replaced him too soon? Too late?

Assignment

Contrast Georgian London and Stuart England.

Assignment

King Williams' War was really two wars. Explain.

Assignment

A. The allied armies led by John Churchill, the 1st Duke of Marlborough, met and defeated every general and every army that King Louis XIV of France could put against them. Born into a family impoverished by the English Civil War, Marlborough ironically learned his trade as a soldier in the French Army. Do wars make great generals or do great generals make great victories?

B. As nation states consolidated their power in the early modern period, Europe witnessed tragic economic dislocations, oppression, and wars leading to waves of terrorism and revolution that mirror our contemporary world situation in striking ways. Compare unrest in the Middle East with Europe in the 18th century.

Assignment

Why were European rulers willing to fight world wars to maintain the status quo?

Assignment

Historian Robert Harris argued that the press, more than anything else, for the first time in history, caused the Seven Year's War (French and Indian War). It inflamed the British public to come to arms against perceived enemies. America experienced a similar event at the end of the Vietnam War, when the press functioned in an opposite spirit, urging America to leave Vietnam. At what point does the press move beyond responsible, free license and into dangerous, irresponsible journalism? Should it be controlled?

Assignment

Why were the British able to supplant the Portuguese, Dutch and Spanish empires in the 17th and 18th centuries and effectively thwart French, Russian and German challenges?

Assignment

Why was English mercantilism so successful?

Assignment

In 1600, the East India Company was the forerunner of the modern multinational. Starting life as a trader in Asian spices, the Company ended its days running Britain's Indian empire. In the process, it shocked its contemporaries with the scale of its violence, corruption and speculation. War, famine, stock-market fixing, they are all a part of the East India Company. The Company's legacy provides compelling lessons on how to ensure the accountability of today's global business. In light of the present problems with multinational corporations, what sort of safeguards should governments establish to control large multi-national corporations like the East India Company?

Assignment

Why did the American colonists win the American Revolution?

Assignment

What aspects of the French Revolution appealed to romantics?

Assignment

In what way was the Revolution Controversy what historian Alfred Cobban calls "perhaps the last real discussion of the fundamentals of politics" in Britain?

Assignment

While the reader will no doubt sympathize with the point of view of these newspaper accounts, offer evidence that the newspaper accounts are prejudicial.

Assignment

What are advantages, and disadvantages, of writing history the way that Carlyle wrote his personal history?

Assignment

Why would a Calvinist have a great deal of trouble with Godwin? Discuss Godwin's view of morality and why it is anti-Christian.

Assignment

What contradiction is evident in Rousseau's thought?

Assignment

How would Burke define these terms: Parliament, government, compromise?

Assignment

A. Summarize Paine's arguments. While Paine was not a confessing Christian, he nonetheless evoked images from the Scriptures. Why, and what are they?

B. Compare and contrast Paine and Burke. At what points do they agree? Disagree?

Assignment

A. Did Napoleon create his own era, or did the era create a Napoleon Bonaparte?

B. Why was the concept of Levée en masse so revolutionary and important?

Assignment

In almost every instance, Napoleon was greatly outnumbered by his allied opponents. In spite of this fact, why did Napoleon win so many battles?

Assignment

A. After defeating the Russians decisively, why did Napoleon still lose the Russian Campaign?

B. Did Napoleon really have a chance to win at Waterloo?

Assignment

Why would De Balzac choose to tell his story from the perspective of an ex-soldier? Why is his audience also important?

Assignment

One historian observed, "The most far-reaching, influential transformation of human culture since the advent of agriculture eight or ten thousand years ago, was the Industrial Revolution of 19th-century Europe. The consequences of this revolution would change irrevocably human labor, consumption, family structure, social structure, and even the very soul and thoughts of the individual." What were some of these technological advances?

Assignment

One historian argues, "The Industrial Revolution was more than technology—impressive as this technology was. What drove the Industrial Revolution were profound social changes, as Europe moved from a primarily agricultural and rural economy to a capitalist and urban economy, from a household, family-based economy to an industry-based economy. This required rethinking social obligations and the structure of the family; the abandonment of the family economy, for instance, was the most dramatic change to the structure of the family that Europe had ever undergone--and we're still struggling with these changes." Why did the abandonment of the family economy have such a radical impact on society?

Assignment

A. Wilberforce invested his life into a cause that never brought him approbation or riches. What cause can you join that is worth a lifetime of effort?

B. Some pro-life proponents argue that abortion is such a heinous crime that the "means justify the end." They openly harass pro-choice proponents and participants. They even commit unlawful acts. Other pro-life proponents are "gradualists" and seek to work through the courts, waiting for the day that legal entities will change laws and end abortion. Which position is most effective?

Assignment

The economist Adam Smith wrote his influential book, *The Wealth of Nations,* which proposed that the only legitimate goal of national government and human activity is the steady increase in the overall wealth of the nation. Why was this a threat to the aristocracy and a boon for early business leaders?

Assignment

A. George IV was a very poor example of probity to his reign. Should he have been impeached?

B. What happens when a leader acts in an immoral way? What happens to a nation whose leadership exhibits these bad choices?

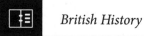
Assignment

Why was King William IV able to survive a British democratic upheaval when so many of his European peers did not?

Assignment

One contemporary describes 19th-century mill girls: "In 1832, our town was little more than a factory village full of textile mills. The employee of choice was single women. Troops of girls came from different parts of New England, and from Canada, and men were employed to collect them at so much a head, and deliver them at the factories. Women were of different ages. Some were not over ten years old; a few were in middle life, but the majority were between the ages of sixteen and twenty-five. They were paid two dollars a week. The working hours of all the girls extended from five o'clock in the morning until seven in the evening. Those of the mill—girls who had homes generally worked from eight to ten months in the year; the rest of the time was spent with parents or friends. A few taught school during the summer months. The most prevailing incentive to labor was to secure the means of education for some male member of the family. To make a gentleman of a brother or a son, to give him a college education, was the dominant thought in the minds of a great many of the better class of mill girls. I have known more than one to give every cent of her wages, month after month, to her brother, that he might get the education necessary to enter some profession. I have known a mother to work years in this way for her boy. I have known women to educate young men by their earnings, who were not sons or relatives. There are many men now living who were helped to an education by the wages of the early mill girls." Do you think hiring mill girls was desirable or a necessary evil?

Assignment

Do you think England did enough to help its Irish neighbor? What responsibilities does a nation have to help another nation? Why?

Assignment

One historian wrote, "In the midst of this tumult, the Victorians were troubled by Time. On the one hand, there was not enough of it: the accelerated pace of change kept people too busy to assimilate the torrent of new ideas and technologies. In the 1880s the essayist F. R. Harrison contended that Victorians were experiencing 'a life lived so full...that we have no time to reflect where we have been and whither we intend to go.' On the other hand, there was too much time: well before Darwin, scientists were showing that vast eons of geological and cosmic development had preceded human history, itself suddenly lengthening due to such discoveries as the Neanderthal skeletons found in 1856." Contrast this description of Victorian England with contemporary America.

Assignment

In pursuit of a just, righteous cause, when (if ever) is violent civil disobedience justified?

Assignment

Albert Einstein, when hearing that sociologists used his theory of physics in sociological theory was horrified. Spencer takes a biological theory (and a bad one at that) and applies it to the sociological realm. What are the dangers of doing that?

Assignment

Do you think that the Industrial Revolution started in England instead of France because England was a Protestant nation? Support your opinion with well-considered arguments.

Assignment

In spite of the fact that the Victorian Age was marked by probity and high moral standards, the Church declined in influence and popularity. Why?

Assignment

Ironically, Victorian England, an intensely religious nation, was completely undermined by Darwinism.

Evolutionary forces decreed that only the fittest should survive in capitalist competition as well as in nature. Applied to nations and races as well as individuals, this theory supported the apparent destiny of England to prosper and rule the world. In the long run, however, this viewpoint was disastrous to England. Explain.

Assignment

Reflect upon the life of Booth in the context of his social ministries. He was not only a solid, anointed evangelist; he was also the best social welfare agent in London. Discuss why this is a winsome combination.

Assignment

Florence Nightingale could care less about women's rights, but in some ways she did more to advance women's rights than Emmeline Pankhurst. How could that be?

Assignment

Like the Americans who invaded Iraq in the early 21st century, the 19th-century British found that using the military to do nation building was difficult if not impossible. What is nation building and why is it so hard to do?

Assignment

Why was the Crimean War fought?

Assignment

Discuss the Indian Mutiny of 1857.

Assignment

Wherever the British went, they established churches and Christian influence. Did this justify the occupation of Afghanistan?

Assignment

What commercial interest did the British have in West Africa?

Assignment

A. Unfortunately, some of Livingstone's children did not appreciate the fact that their father was away when their mother died. They accused him of choosing his calling over his wife. What do you think?

B. Was David Livingston a Christian advancing the Gospel first and British civilization second, or was he a British citizen advancing British culture first and the Gospel second?

Assignment

Why did British forces often lose individual battles but ultimately won colonial wars?

Assignment

Speculate (the reading does not offer an answer) upon why the British persevered in their domination of interior Africa that had marginal commercial interest?

Assignment

Why were the Boers so hard to beat?

Assignment

What were the roots of the Boxer Rebellion?

Assignment

What contributions did George V make to the British monarchy?

Assignment

The music hall was the most popular and defining institution of early 20th century English history. It entertained the masses, it spoke soothing platitudes to the poor, and it showcased the fashions and traditions of Britain. What popular institution would today define our nation? Why?

Assignment

England, at the beginning of the 20th century, made an honest effort to improve the lives of their citizens. However, ultimately, most of these efforts failed. Why?

Assignment

What are the inherent dangers of a social welfare state?

Assignment

To Nietzsche God is dead in the hearts of modern men— killed by rationalism and science. How should Christians reply to Nietzsche?

Assignment

Shelley warns her readers of relying too much on science. The end result could very well be a "monster." Likewise, many modernists, suspicious of tradition but excited about the advances in technology have a love/hate relationship with science. Why does modernism embrace and reject science, both at the same time?

Assignment

Why was Franz Joseph one of the main, if not primary reason for World War I?

Assignment

How did alliances contribute to the causes of World War I?

Assignment

In naval matters, why doesn't Grey want Germany to have parity with England?

Assignment

The last 20 years of the 19th century, 1880 to 1900, were characterized by an immense optimism. It was thought that public health, invention, the telegraph, the telephone, ultimately the wireless and the radio, were going to civilize human life in a way that it had never been civilized before. And, then, all of a sudden, what happens in World War I is horrible, nothing like what was expected. How might a Christian explain these contrasts?

Assignment

The First World War changed the world, and was a moment of passage between the 19th century and 20th century, and encouraged the of rise modernity. Discuss how the war truly ended the Victorian Age and started Europe on the path to modernity.

Assignment

Even after 20,000 men died in the first 24 hours of the Battle of the Somme, the British high command continued the battle for 5 months more. Why?

Assignment

The British were the most innovative belligerents of the war. They were the first to develop the airplane and the tank as serious tactical weapons. In your opinion, why were the British so innovative?

Assignment

Assuming you were Winston Churchill's "agent" or benefactor, from this brief biography, what vocation would you advise him to pursue?

Assignment

A. What was the outcome of the Versailles Treaty?

B. Why did the Treaty of Versailles satisfy no one?

Assignment

Verdun was one of the most horrendous battles of world history. Nothing is quite its equal (except the second day in the 1864 Battle of Spotsylvania Courthouse between the Confederacy and the Union). Nearly a million men died at Verdun. Why would two civilized nations fight such a battle?

Assignment

How was the affect of the influenza epidemic exacerbated by World War I?

Assignment

Why did London recover so quickly after World War I?

Assignment

What new problems emerged in England after World War I?

Assignment

Why were totalitarian regimes so popular after World War I?

Assignment

Why did post-World War I England have such an ambivalent view of Hitler?

Assignment

Why was Japan such a serious threat to England?

Assignment

What three "Englands" does Priestly find in 1933?

Assignment

Compare these three monarchs: Henry VIII, Queen Elizabeth I, and Queen Elizabeth II.

Assignment

In defense of poor Neville Chamberlain, what could he do? England was not ready to fight a war and his decision did give England two more years to prepare for war. Also, appeasement of sorts had worked well enough with Hitler in 1936 when he desisted from conquests after the Austrian Anschluss. What do you think?

Assignment

Would England have won World War II without American intervention?

Assignment

Why did the Soviets lose the Cold War to England and her allies?

Assignment

What precipitated the Cold War between England and the Soviet Union?

Assignment

Even though England won World War II, it lost almost all its empire. Why?

Assignment

Predict the future of England in the following areas: Social, economic, and technological.

Chapter Exam Section

Exam Questions: 60-100 words

A. Great Britain was conquered several times by several different people groups and nations. Why? What allure do these islands offer invaders? (**33 points**)

B. Apparently early England was ruled by a priestly class (i.e., the druids). G. K. Chesterton wrote, "They [the Britons) were apparently ruled by that terrible thing, a pagan priesthood. Stones now shapeless yet arranged in symbolic shapes bear witness to the order and labour of those that lifted them." Given that fact, what societal tendencies do you surmise emerge in this religion-governed society? (**33 points**)

C. Normally religion arises before technology. In fact, technology often is a real threat to religion. For example, the rise of the scientific revolution threatened the Roman Catholic Church. In England, though, technology preceded religion. The Celts conquered England to obtain English tin and later developed iron weapons and implements. Technology was in full bloom when the druids emerged. Why? Why in this culture did religion emerge after technology, instead of vice versa? **(34 points)**

Exam Questions: 60-100 words (50 points each)

A. Explain this quote from English scholar G. K. Chesterton: "Rome itself, which had made all that strong world, was the weakest thing in it. The centre had been growing fainter and fainter, and now the centre disappeared. Rome had as much freed the world as ruled it, and now she could rule no more . . . A loose localism was the result rather than any conscious intellectual mutiny. There was anarchy, but there was no rebellion. For rebellion must have a principle, and therefore an authority . . . . The Empire did decline, but it did not fall. It remains to this hour."

B. Roman rule in other parts of the Empire was abhorred while it existed and applauded when it left. To Britons, however, Roman rule was the "Golden Age." In spite of their Germanic heritage, the Britons wanted to be Roman more than Germanic (i.e., like the invading German Saxons). Why?

Exam Questions: 60-100 Words (50 points each)

A. Advances were taking place in technology. In England an advance in technology came with the use of water wheels. Windmills also appeared. Englishmen were using cranks—one of the most important inventions in the history of mankind. These advances had a profound effect on Great Britain. Discuss how advances in technology have affected your life over the last 20 years.

B. Pope Gregory urged Anglo-Saxon King Aethelberht to destroy the temples and practices of rival religions. King Aethelberht did not take Pope Gregory's advice. He allowed the pagan temples to be left standing if they were well built. Aethelberht also kept pagan feast days. Thus, in England the Saxon's spring festival of the goddess Eostre would become a Christian festival called Easter. This is a form of syncretism. What are the dangers of syncretism?

Exam Questions: 60-100 Words (50 points each)

A. Discuss the impact that the Magna Carta had on world history.

B. Thomas Becket, Archbishop of Canterbury, died on a cold December evening as he struggled on the steps of his altar. Most people then, and now, feel that King Henry II was responsible for Becket's murder. Becket first met King Henry II in 1154. Henry and Becket were friends from the beginning. Henry appointed Becket to the highest church office in England: the Archbishop of Canterbury. Then things changed. Becket's allegiance appropriately moved from king to Church. Henry II did not like this at all. Things came to a head when Henry usurped Church judicial power. Becket and Henry II were now enemies. Becket, afraid for his life, fled to France.

Then, there was a sort of reconciliation in 1170 when King Henry and Becket met in Normandy. Becket crossed the Channel returning to his post at Canterbury. Earlier, while in France, Becket had excommunicated the Bishops of London and Salisbury for their support of King Henry. Henry now expected Becket to forgive these wayward bishops. Becket outraged King Henry II again by refusing to do so. Henry is purported to have said to some knights, "What sluggards, what cowards have I brought up in my court, who care nothing for their allegiance to their lord? Who will rid me of this meddlesome priest?" Four knights slew Becket at the altar of his church. The whole thing unnerved the king and he repented of his loose talk. Contrast this story with the story of King Herod beheading John the Baptist.

Exam Questions: 60-100 Words (50 points each)

A. When should a Christian obey the civil authorities and when should Christians disobey civil authorities?

B. Historian Keith Thomas argued that Roman Catholicism filled a gap, addressed a need. Thomas, himself an agnostic, argued that Roman Catholicism, at best, quelled the superstitious fears of people. Obviously, Thomas had a jaded view of Roman Catholicism. But his point was that Protestantism, particular English Protestantism, was unable to allay the fears and superstitutions of ordinary people. In other words, Protestantism could not flourish until science dispelled any need for superstitious explanations for reality. Do you agree?

Exam Questions: 60-100 Words (50 points each)

A. Agree or disagree with the following quote by G. K. Chesterton. "Wooden clichés about the birth of the British Empire and the spacious days of Queen Elizabeth have not merely obscured but contradicted the crucial truth. From such phrases one would fancy that England, in some imperial fashion, now first realized that she was great. It would be far truer to say that she now first realized that she was small."

B. After the English defeated the Spanish Armada, Elizabeth claimed that God delivered England because He loved Protestants and hated the Roman Catholics. Respond to her claim.

Exam Question: 60-100 Words (100 points)

Most historians argue that the Elizabethan Age is the apex of British civilization. Advances in science, art, and technology occurred in every way. England and Protestantism triumphed. But G. K. Chesterton has another view. React to this statement in his *A Short History of England*: "For the splendour of the Elizabethan age, which is always spoken of as a sunrise, was in many ways a sunset. Whether we regard it as the end of the Renascence or the end of the old medieval civilization, no candid critic can deny that its chief glories ended with it. Let the reader ask himself what strikes him specially in the Elizabethan magnificence, and he will generally find it is something of which there were at least traces in medieval times, and far fewer traces in modern times. The Elizabethan drama is like one of its own tragedies—its tempestuous torch was soon to be trodden out by the Puritans. It is needless to say that the chief tragedy was the cutting short of the comedy; for the comedy that came to England after the Restoration was by comparison both foreign and frigid."

Exam Questions: 60-100 Words (50 points each)

A. Little could be done to cure diseases because no one really knew what caused them. Some people blamed the stars. Some thought gluttony was the cause. Some blamed England's cold, damp climate. During the widespread outbreaks of the disease such as the plague, ethnic groups, like the Jews, were accused of poisoning wells. Amazingly, the real cause occurred to no one. It was not until the invention of the microscope in the next century that scientists could see what caused the disease and how it was spread. Doctors and city officials knew the plague was highly contagious, but had no idea how it was spread. They thought, for instance, that it was spread by dogs and cats. So they killed all their pets—and it was the cats who were killing the real culprits: rats! Elizabethans knew the bodies of the dead should be avoided, that their houses should be shut up, (or quarantined) and that garbage should be burned. However, no family would burn down its house. Their orders were mostly ignored. Elizabethan government was "insufficiently organized to carry out with success an strict set of unpopular orders . . . the authorities were forced to sit with folded hands until the plague had run its course." As a result, between one-third and one-half of the population of England died. What happens to a society of 4 million people that loses 1 to 1.5 million citizens in one year?

B. The Elizabethans seriously tried to ameliorate the plight of the poor, and, in some cases to remove poverty altogether. No other society had tried to do that. Why did the Elizabethans try?

Exam Question: 60-100 Words (100 points)

Answer the following question. During this time in English history the Anglicans despised the Puritans. The Puritans detested the Quakers and everyone hated the Baptists. Why do committed Christians nonetheless fight among themselves?

Exam Questions: 60-100 words

A. React to the following criticism of Puritanism. Speaking of Puritanism in relation to art, Mr. Gutzon Borglum said: "Puritanism has made us self-centered and hypocritical for so long, that sincerity and reverence for what is natural in our impulses have been fairly bred out of us, with the result that there can be neither truth nor individuality in our art." Mr. Borglum might have added that Puritanism has made life itself impossible. More than art, more than astheticism, life represents beauty in a thousand variations; it is indeed, a gigantic panorama of eternal change. Puritanism, on the other hand, rests on a fixed and immovable conception of life; it is based on the Calvinistic idea that life is a curse, imposed upon man by the wrath of God. In order to redeem himself man must do constant penance, must repudiate every natural and healthy impulse, and turn his back on joy and beauty. **(34 Points)**

B. G. K. Chesterton wrote, "Thus the Puritans, as their name implies, were primarily enthusiastic for what they thought was pure religion; frequently they wanted to impose it on others; sometimes they only wanted to be free to practice it themselves; but in no case can justice be done to what was finest in their characters, as well as first in their thoughts, if we never by any chance ask what 'it' was that they wanted to impose or to practice. Now, there was a great deal that was very fine about many of the Puritans, which is almost entirely missed by the modern admirers of the Puritans. They are praised for things which they either regarded with indifference or more often detested with frenzy—such as religious liberty. And yet they are quite insufficiently understood, and are even undervalued, in their logical case for the things they really did care about—such as Calvinism. We make the Puritans picturesque in a way they would violently repudiate, in novels and plays they would have publicly burnt. We are interested in everything about them, except the only thing in which they were interested at all." What were the Puritans "interested in?" **(33 Points)**

C. Most historians argue that Cromwell was a self-serving, mean man who only used religion to advance his pragmatic causes. Historian Antonia Fraser, on the other hand, described Cromwell as an often misunderstood and demonized Puritanical zealot. Oliver Cromwell rose from humble beginnings to spearhead the rebellion against King Charles I, who was beheaded in 1649, and led his soldiers into the last battle against the Royalists and King Charles II at Worcester, ending the Civil War in 1651. Fraser shows how England's prestige and prosperity grew under Cromwell, reversing the decline it had suffered since Queen Elizabeth I's death. Fraser, in effect, humanized the righteous and arrogant Lord Protector, presenting him as "a fallible, paradoxical and essentially melancholic figure." But, still, she didn't downplay his cruelties: his joy at the execution of King Charles, and his vendetta against the Irish. Fraser, we contended, made Cromwell out "to be a kinder, more patient and conciliatory man than one had hitherto suspected . . . a man rooted in the English countryside." Which Cromwell do you think really existed? **(33 Points)**

Exam Questions: 60-100 words

A. Christian dissenters or radicals in the Commonwealth, most of whom were Puritans, or Presbyterians, were confronted by a dilemma. On one hand, there was a strong belief in the evolution of truth, continuous revelation. "The daily progress of the light of truth," said Puritan poet Milton, "is productive far less of disturbance to the church, than of illumination and edification. Through revelation of new truths to believers, traditional Christianity could be adapted to the needs of a new age; the everlasting gospel within responded more easily and swiftly to the pressures of the environment than did traditions of the church or the literal text. History is a gradual progress towards total revelation of truth." The second principle argued for a reliance on the Holy Spirit within one, on one's own experienced truth as against traditional truths handed down by others. All of this "truth," of course, was to be weighed against Scripture that was timeless, immutable, and inerrant. The problem was that some of the Puritan radicals gravitated to a form of antinomianism—that is, lawlessness. If a person is motivated by "new revelation" and subject only "to the Holy Spirit," why not experience new, perhaps wicked things? Thus, small-town Puritans who would never think of flogging a person to death for seditious behavior found themselves doing it in the Commonwealth! How does a Christian balance the need for tradition and specific revelation with an emerging, reforming revelation (See Christopher Hill's, *The World Turned Upside Down*)? **(33 Points)**

B. Christian leaders in the Commonwealth were on the horns of a dilemma. On one hand, they fervently embraced the Word of God as the principle on which to build and to maintain a healthy society. On the other hand, they relied on sinful people to run that godly society. Ultimately many individuals grew in Christ because of the efforts of the Puritan leadership but the society itself self-destructed. Why? **(34 Points)**

C. Charles I refused to repent of his Royalist views and even refused to desist from encouraging rebellion. Therefore, Cromwell felt he had no choice but to execute King Charles I. Did he make the right choice? **(33 Points)**

Exam Discussion Questions

A. During the 17th century, England was beset by three epidemics of the bubonic plague, each outbreak claiming a third of the population of London and other urban centers. Surveying a wide range of responses to these epidemics—sermons, medical tracts, pious exhortations, satirical pamphlets, and political commentary—so called "plague writing" in early modern England bring to life the many and complex ways Londoners made sense of such unspeakable devastation. The 17th century English did not have any other way to express their consternation, fear, and grief. Historian Ernest B. Gilman argues that the plague writing of the period attempted unsuccessfully to rationalize the catastrophic and that its failure to account for the plague as an instrument of divine justice fundamentally threatened the core of Christian belief. Plague writing holds up a mirror to reflect our own condition in the age of AIDS, super viruses, multidrug resistant-tuberculosis, and the hovering threat of a global flu pandemic. Gilman says that 17th century English leaders argued that the plague was God's judgment on English immoral lasciviousness. Could they be right? If so, would the present AIDS epidemic be a similar judgment? **(50 Points)**

B. Some historians refer to Charles II as the "gambling king." Explain. **(25 Points)**

C. Scotland and Wales joined Great Britain and were part of the United Kingdom. Not Ireland. Why? **(25 Points)**

Exam Questions: 60-100 Words (100 points)

The Glorious Revolution was a great victory—for Protestants! From this moment forward, Protestants alone could rule in England. Roman Catholicism became even a more dangerous religion to follow. Catholics were denied the right to vote and sit in the Westminster Parliament for over 100 years after this and the monarch was forbidden to be Catholic or marry a Catholic, thus ensuring the Protestant succession. There is, in some crises, a "piling on effect." That is, groups in disagreement can find agreement if they can blame someone else for their troubles! Some of that occurred in the Glorious Revolution. Imagine how you would feel if you were Roman Catholic and lived in 17th-century England. How "glorious was this revolution?" Why are British officials so afraid of Roman Catholics?

Exam Discussion Questions

A. G.K. Chesterton in his *A Short History of England* writes, "The transformation through which the external relations of England passed at the end of the seventeenth century is symbolized by two very separate and definite steps; the first the accession of a Dutch king and the second the accession of a German king. In the first were present all the features that can partially make an unnatural thing natural. In the second we have the condition in which even those effecting it can hardly call it natural, but only call it necessary. William of Orange was like a gun dragged into the breach of a wall; a foreign gun indeed, and one fired in a quarrel more foreign than English, but still a quarrel in which the English, and especially the English aristocrats, could play a great part. George of Hanover was simply something stuffed into a hole in the wall by English aristocrats, who practically admitted that they were simply stopping it with rubbish. In many ways William, cynical as he was, carried on the legend of the greater and grimmer Puritanism. He was in private conviction a Calvinist; and nobody knew or cared what George was except that he was not a Catholic. He was at home the partly republican magistrate of what had once been a purely republican experiment, and among the cleaner if colder ideals of the seventeenth century. George was when he was at home pretty much what the King of the Cannibal Islands was when he was at home—a savage personal ruler scarcely logical enough to be called a despot. William was a man of acute if narrow intelligence; George was a man of no intelligence. Above all, touching the immediate effect produced, William was married to a Stuart, and ascended the throne hand-in-hand with a Stuart; he was a familiar figure, and already a part of our royal family. With George there entered England something that had scarcely been seen there before; something hardly mentioned in mediæval or Renascence wons a Hottentot—the barbarian from beyond the Rhine." Paraphrase this quote. **(75 points)**

B. Chesterton says, "The reign of Queen Anne, which covers the period between these two foreign kings, is therefore the true time of transition. It is the bridge between the time when the aristocrats were at least weak enough to call in a strong man to help them, and the time when they were strong enough deliberately to call in a weak man who would allow them to help themselves. To symbolize is always to simplify, and to simplify too much; but the whole may be well symbolized as the struggle of two great figures, both gentlemen and men of genius, both courageous and clear about their own aims, and in everything else a violent contrast at every point. One of them was Henry St. John, Lord Bolingbroke; the other was John Churchill, the famous and infamous Duke of Marlborough. The story of Churchill is primarily the story of the Revolution and how it succeeded; the story of Bolingbroke is the story of the Counter-Revolution and how it failed." Paraphrase this quote. Do you agree? (**25 points**)

Exam Questions: 60-100 Words (50 points each)

A. Was King George a "Royal Brute" as American patriots claimed? Or was he, as others believed, "the father of the people?" Was George Washington a scurrilous traitor, as all the king's supporters claimed? Or should we remember and celebrate him as "the father of his country?" Who was right?

B. Both George II and III, with all their faults, were devoted, faithful husbands. In light our American scandals among political leaders, how do you assess the importance of this morality? Would you prefer to have a moral leader who stands against your political views? Or would you prefer to have an immoral leader who agrees with your political views? Increasingly, Americans have chosen the latter over the former. What do you think?

Exam Questions: 60-100 Words (50 points each)

A. Why did England essentially win the conflicts that were fought between 1690–1763?

B. In spite of a consensus that the English had subjugated the Irish, many fought loyally in the British Army. Throughout this period, the Irish brigades in France and Spain participated in conflicts ranging from the wars of the Spanish and Austrian Succession to the Napoleonic Wars. Why?

Exam Discussion Questions

A. Define mercantilism and discuss whether or not it worked. (**34 Points**)

B. In what ways did the 1600 arrangement with the East India Company benefit the East India Company and the British government? **(33 Points)**

C. Were the American colonists justified in their revolution? Could not their grievances have been satisfied in peaceful ways? **(33 Points)**

Exam Questions: 60-100 Words (50 points each)

A. From your own memory of an historical event (e.g., September 11, 2001), discuss how public opinion has shifted back and forth, both in sympathy and in condemnation.

B. English writer Charles Caleb wrote, "The consequences of things are not always proportionate to the apparent magnitude of those events that have produced them. Thus the American Revolution, from which little was expected, produced much; but the French Revolution, from which much was expected, produced little." Respond to this statement.

Complete the chart (100 points, 25 points/philosopher)

Philosopher	Religion	Government	Revolution	Violence
William Godwin				
Jean Jacques Rousseau				
Thomas Paine				
Edmund Burke				

Exam Question 100-150 Words (100 points)

Napoleon described his career this way: "I closed the gulf of anarchy and brought order out of chaos. I rewarded merit regardless of birth or wealth, wherever I found it. I abolished feudalism and restored equality to all regardless of religion and before the law. I fought the decrepit monarchies of the Old Regime because the alternative was the destruction of all this. I purified the Revolution." What do you think of his assessment?

Exam Question (100 points)

Pretend that you own an 1840 Liverpool, England, cotton cloth-producing business. You are providing income for 20 local families. You give cottage industries raw cotton that you have imported from the United States. They process it and give back to you rolls of cotton cloth. You then export it to cloth-makers in Birmingham, England. You have heard of a new cotton gin and spinning jenny that a competitor has begun to use. You aren't too worried because, while your competitor's cloth is cheaper, you feel yours is much better. However, within a few months you realize that the consumer prefers the cheaper cloth to your product. Or at least better quality cotton cloth is not worth the extra cost to most consumers. Besides, your major vendor, the Birmingham cloth-maker, has cancelled your order and is buying from your competitor. You have to admit that you are losing business. Your business plan tells you that you can recoup your capital expenditures that modernization will cost you within a year. However, you will only need half the workers you presently employ. Several of your employees are old and will not be able to obtain other employment. What will you do?

Exam Questions: 60-100 Words

A. Organized religion was much more important in the 19th century than it is today. Nevertheless in 1851 a survey showed that only about 40 percent of the population were at church or chapel on a given Sunday. Even allowing for those who were ill or could not make it for some other reason it meant that half the population did not go to church. Certainly many of the poor had little or no contact with the church. In 1881 a similar survey showed only about one-third of the population at church on a given Sunday. In the late 19th century organized religion was in decline. In your opinion, why? **(50 Points)**

B. In the early 19th century poor people often had cesspits, which were not emptied very often. Later in the century many people used earth closets (a bucket toilet with a box containing granulated sand in it. When you pulled a lever clay or sand covered the contents of the bucket). In the early 19th century only wealthy people had flushing lavatories. However in the late 19th century they became common. This invention, however, caused more problems. Why? (**25 Points**)

C. At the end of the 19th century more than 25 percent of the population was living at or below subsistence level. In your opinion, why? (**25 Points**)

Exam Question (100 points)

React to the following quote: "The whole meaning of Victorian England is lost if it is thought of as a country of stuffy complacency and black top-hatted moral priggery. Its frowsty crinolines and dingy hansom cabs, its gas-lit houses and over-ornate draperies, concealed a people engaged in a tremendously exciting adventure--the daring experiment of fitting industrial man into a democratic society," historian David Thompson, 1950.

Exam Questions: 100-150 Words (50 points each)

A. Agree or disagree with this statement: "Never since the beginning of Time was there, that we hear or read of, so intensely self-conscious a Society. Our whole relations to the Universe and to our fellow-man have become an Inquiry, a Doubt." Thomas Carlyle, a Victorian Englishman, 1831.

B. What is *Punch* magazine trying to say about William Booth? Do you agree with its outlook?

Exam Questions: 100-150 Words (50 points each)

A. The First Afghan War provided the clear lesson to the British authorities that while it may be relatively straightforward to invade Afghanistan it is wholly impracticable to occupy the country or attempt to impose a government not welcomed by the inhabitants. The only result will be failure and great expense in treasure and lives. What implications did this have for the American Al-Qaida War in Afghanistan, 2001?

B. Why is Afghan so difficult for outside nations to subjugate?

Exam Questions: 100-150 Words (50 points each)

A. Iranian President Ahmadinejad's preoccupation with the coming of a Islamic messiah figure, the Mahdi, is raising concerns that a nuclear-armed Islamic republic could trigger the kind of global disaster that he envisions will set the stage for the end of the world. While Mahmoud Ahmadinejad has been making headlines lately by questioning whether the Holocaust actually happened, by suggesting Israel should be moved to Europe and by demanding the Jewish state be wiped off the face of the earth, his apocalyptic religious zealotry has received less attention. In light of the British experience with Islamic extremist at the end of the 19th century, what advice would you give the President of the United States?

B. In the Zulu Wars occurred one of the worst disasters of the Colonial era when over thirteen hundred British troops and their African allies were killed. In the aftermath the Zulu reserves mounted a raid on the British border post at Rorke's Drift, which was held by just 145 men (as portrayed in the movie *Zulu*). After ten hours of ferocious fighting, the Zulu were driven off. Should the British simply have left South Africa at that point?

Exam Question (100 points)

Not all aspects of "imperialism"—whether practiced by Britain in the 19th century or the US today—are necessarily pernicious. Name a few good things that Britain brought to the world through its empire.

Exam Question: 60-100 Words (100 points)

Discuss why the following piece of art is quintessentially modern.

Exam Question

A. King George V of Great Britain was first cousin through his mother to Tsar Nicholas II, the last tsar of Russia, and first cousin through his father to Kaiser Wilhelm II, the last Kaiser of Germany. In fact, by the time he was 31 his grandmother Queen Victoria had ensured that he was related by blood or marriage to every royal family in Europe. Wilhelm took Germany to war with Britain, but during the war and even afterwards he couldn't shake off his life-long addiction to all things English: he read English papers, drank English tea, laughed at P.G. Wodehouse, and wore a tie pin with a miniature of his dearest Grandmamma, Queen Victoria. Why did the cousins allow war to come to Europe? **(25 points)**

B. One historian argues, "Once Europe had entered the age of the million-man army, which it did after the general adoption of systems of universal conscription at the end of the 1870s, war became too complicated for the politicians to understand, let alone control. Every army now had its general staff system in which military technicians made war plans and mobilization schedules and schemes for logistical support and schedules for weapons development and testing that were bewildering and baffling to the layman; and in time of crisis the soldiers, called into conference, could be counted on to demand the immediate implementation of their plans and to argue that the alternative would be disaster. The "use-them-or-lose-them" mentality of the soldiers meant that the normal processes of diplomatic negotiation and delay were overwhelmed by arguments of military urgency and expediency. Everyone remembered how the Prussians had overwhelmed the Austrians in 1866 and the French in 1870 because of their superior use of the railways to ferry large numbers of troops to the front with speed and efficiency." What caused the War? Nationalism? Militarism? Alliances? **(75 points)**

Exam Question: 80-100 Words (100 points)

British historian John Keegan argues, "The English officer class came to the war as innocents. They'd been brought up on high-minded Greek and Roman poetry and prose, and it was a frightful shock to them to discover that their imagination of war, which had been fed by the classical literature of war, was incorrect. The war wasn't brave and heroic, it was pretty horrible and nasty and dirty, and you were more concerned about keeping dry and keeping warm than you were about closing with the enemy. And, people got killed all the time without ever seeing the enemy. And, people died in squalid ways. And, people were frightened. And, people were cowardly. This was a very, very great shock to this over-educated officer class." Besides the fact that there were so many casualties, why was this war so "shocking?"

Exam Question: 80-100 Words (100 points)

Pretend that you had the power to design a just peace treaty for World War I. What would you do? In your answer, discuss territory changes, war guilt, and reparations.

Exam Question: 60-100 Words (100 points)

In retrospect, how should England have responded to nascent German, Italian, and Japanese totalitarianism?

Dates (25 points)

Mark these events in the order they occurred:

_____ D-Day

_____ The London Blitz

_____ The Munich Conference

_____ Pearl Harbor

_____ Winston Churchill is elected prime minister

Exam Question: 60-100 Words (75 points)

Based solely on our above discussion, why was England never invaded by Germany?

Exam Question: 80-100 Words (100 points)

Looking back over this year, if you could go back in time, in what part of British history would you like to live? Why?

Answer Key

⚷ Discussion Question Answer Key

Chapter 1

Lesson 1

Britons were a warrior, nomadic people who had no use for writing. Besides, in a highly religious culture, based on motif and ritual, writing was not necessary. This did not mean that the Britons were not intelligent people. Scops and minstrels would tell and retell stories about heroes (e.g., *Beowulf*) that would not be written down until centuries later but the stories and legends were in the culture.

Lesson 2

The ancient Englishmen (Scots, Picts, Angles, Britons, and Celts) were farmers living in small communities. Cattle and horses were an obvious sign of wealth and prestige. Cereal crops included wheat, barley, oats and rye. Vegetables included kale, cabbage, onions and leeks, peas and beans, turnips and carrots. Plants such as wild garlic, nettles and watercress may have been gathered in the wild. The pastoral economy meant that hides and leather were readily available. Wool was the main source of clothing, and flax was also common. Fish, shellfish, seals and whales were exploited along coasts and rivers. The importance of domesticated animals argues that meat and milk products were a major part of the diet of ordinary people, while wealthier Britons would have eaten a diet rich in meat from farming and hunting. The Picts lived mostly in the north and northeast and they spoke a kind of Celtic language which was lost completely. The Scots originally came from Ireland. The Scots were Celtic settlers who moved into the western Highlands from Ireland in the fourth century. The third group was the Britons, who inhabited the Lowlands and what is England. The Picts were excellent warriors and the Romans called them "Picti" (The Painted ones) since most of the times they went into battle completely naked to show their tattooed bodies. They were in fact Celts, the ancestors of the people who built the stone circles. The Picts inherited their rights, their names and property from their mothers. The Angles: came from northern Germany and settled first in the south east of England and they helped the Romans to keep their possession of Britannia. In the fifth century they invaded England and created their own kingdom, Anglia. They were tough and brave warriors. The Britons occupied the west part of the Lowlands from Clyde, over Hadrian's Wall and to the present Lake District.

Lesson 3

A. Of all aspects of the social and religious life of the Celts, one that has found itself shrouded in mystery and speculation is that of the druids. The priestly class of the Celts, and their role in everyday life, has become a matter of contention among scholars. The druids carried out the religious functions of tribal life. They conducted the sacrifices to the gods and goddesses, and upheld the teachings of the Celtic religions. But the druids were also philosophers, medical doctors, natural scientists, and judges. Druids conducted schools, from which many people from outside the Celtic world studied, including many Greeks and Romans. Not only were the schools set up for the study of religion, but for the development of scientific study, law, and philosophic study. The course of study for druidic students was close to 20 years. Students came from all sections of Celtic society. The basis of the word druid is one of controversy. Most likely, it came from the Celtic word for oak, *dru*, and was combined with the word *wid*, or knowledge, rendering a word literally meaning "oak knowledge." The actual meaning was that it was someone whose knowledge was great. The oak was a tree that was very important in Celtic life, even to Christian times. The name Kildare, which was the site of both a druidic school and a Christian church, means the church of the oak in Irish. Druids, according to Julius Caesar, were trained in "international" law. The judgment of a druid could stop a potential war between tribes, because the judgment and moral authority of the druid was greater than the tribal chieftain. The druids had the authority to render legal decisions, which were binding on all parties. They decided boundary disputes, inheritance questions, sentences for murder. If their decisions were not followed by one party or the other, then that person was excluded from the activities of the tribe and society. According to Caesar, "All people leave their company; avoid their presence and speech, lest they should be involved in some of the ill consequences of the situation. They can get no redress for injury, and hold no post of honor." Such acts of exclusion and shunning in a society noted for its interdependence on people could be close to a death sentence on such a person. Druidic teachings held that the soul was immortal. There was no real difference between the world of the present and the afterlife. Druidic teachings had an influence on many of the Greek philosophers. However, one Greek writer claimed that the slave of Pythagoras, who also taught the immortality of the soul, went to the Celtic lands, and gave his teacher's philosophy to the druids. The druids were physicians. They treated with both herbs and potions, and performed surgery. There are reports of cesarian births among Celtic doctors, as well as the repairing of wounds by sewing them. Brain surgery has been reported; in fact, in a Brighton museum, there is a human skull that had two holes drilled into the top of the skull, and that it had healed.Each tribe had to maintain a hospital, which was staffed by the druids and their students. The druids were also seers and practiced magic. The use of releasing hares and birds to predict the future was well known. The sacrifice of animals also provided the druids with visions of the future (www.angelfire. com/wi/THECELTS/druids.html).

B. As one pastor explained, "The origins of Halloween are Celtic in tradition and have to do with observing the end of summer sacrifices to gods in druidic tradition. In what is now Britain and France, it was the beginning of the Celtic year, and they believed Samhain, the lord of death, sent evil spirits abroad to attack humans, who could escape only by assuming disguises and looking like evil spirits themselves. The waning of the sun and the approach of dark winter made the evil spirits rejoice and play nasty tricks. Believe it or not, most of our Halloween practices can be traced back to these old pagan rites and superstitions." Therefore it would be wrong for Christians to celebrate Halloween.

Lesson 4

Prehistoric Britons lived in sturdy wooden roundhouses. Depending on the climate, most domestic life would have occurred within the roundhouse. The main focus of the interior of the house was the central open-hearth fire. This open fireplace cooked food and provided warmth and light. The fire was maintained 24 hours a day. A bronze cauldron (large pot) was held up by a tripod and attached with an adjustable chain. The ordinary basic cooking pots would have been made by hand from the local clay and came in varying rounded shapes, occasionally with simple incised decoration. Bread would have been an important part of any meal, and was made from stone ground flour. No doubt Britons loved milk and other dairy products but seemed to dislike vegetables. Everything happened inside the one-room house. The interior of the house was an ideal place for the drying and preservation of food. Smoke and heat from the constant fire smoked meat. Occasional round stones are found that doubled as game pieces and slingshot ammunition. Britons, even children, men and women, wore close-fitting pants, with a long tunic of either linen or wool, held at the waist with a belt. Over this would have been a cloak that

was fastened at the shoulder with a brooch. The textiles were dyed bright colors and were woven with striped or checked patterns. These colors and patterns no doubt communicated clan ties. Both women and men grew their hair long, sometimes plaited, and that the men sported either beards or moustaches, which they also grew long (British Museum).

Chapter 2

Lesson 1

Like all soldiers, Roman soldiers stationed at Hadrian's Wall spent long hours guarding the northern frontier. Letters and other memorabilia attest to the fact that Roman soldiers performing this duty were terribly bored. At the same time, there were days, even weeks, when these soldiers were required to battle fierce, attacking warriors. It must have been terrifying to see tattooed Picts running toward you with battle axes! Occasionally, but rarely, Roman legions would journey north of the Hadrian's Wall to reconnoiter. These must have been particularly stressful times! Roman soldiers, like all soldiers, enjoyed times of rest and relaxation at local English cities. They would spend hours relaxing in Roman baths, the preferred luxury of every Roman!

Lesson 2

King Arthur is an epic hero. Many epic heroes are recurring characters in the legends of their nativeculture. Epic heroes have no superpowers, but are smart, brave, and have fears but overcome them to protect their families, and countries. An epic hero can also be a warrior of some sort who performs extraordinary tasks that most find difficult. This hero is loyal, smart, and brave. The epic hero is also typically joined by others, who will initially be rejected from the group for their own safety, thus embodying selflessness, a commonly valued trait in English society. King Arthur, and his knights, are brave but sensitive. Reckless but careful. Bold but reflective. Above all, they are absolutely intrepid and honest in everything that they do.

Lesson 3

No one knows for sure if there really was a King Arthur. Most historians, however, believe there really was a Briton King named Arthur, or a combination of Briton kings whose exploits were summed up in the life of one man. Arthur was allegedly the son of King Pendragon, a Briton Welsh King during the Roman occupation.

Legend states that the departing Roman army asked Arthur to protect Britons from the warring Anglo-Saxons pouring into England. Obviously the "legend" of King Arthur contains many untrue elements, but, clearly there was an actual historical Briton king, or group of kings, who led Britons in their fight against the Anglo-Saxon invaders. It is more difficult to believe the stories connected to Camelot, which have an air of exaggeration.

Lesson 4

Rome wisely built roads and bridges to hasten the flow of troops from places of strength to places of weakness. Roman military leaders took advantage of the interior defensive line—that is, they maintained a marginal military force behind a formidable physical barrier (e.g., Hadrian's Wall) and, when there was a problem, they would shift forces from point to point.

Chapter 3

Lesson 1

A. Small in number, they were nonetheless able to conquer all of Britain in one generation. The Britons were disorganized and fighting among themselves. English waterways and Roman roads, encouraged Anglo-Saxon expansion from initial coastal settlements. At the same time, the great plague of the sixth century decimated the Britons.

B. While Roman Christianity fitted itself into the molds of the municipal institutions of the empire, Celtic Christianity had grown out of the tribal system of the peoples who had embraced it. Although not heretical, the Celtic church differed from Rome in the way the monks cut their hair, in its reckoning of the date of Easter, and, most important, in its organization, which emphasized the clans of Ireland rather than the highly centralized Roman Catholic Church.

Lesson 2

In the midst of so much diversity, the Church was a unifying agent among divergent Anglo-Saxon social elements.

Lesson 3

A. London was difficult to defend and it was full of pagan influences (e.g., Mithraism).

B. He was the first Anglo-Saxon king to unify divergent groups in England. King Alfred the Great (849, ruled 871–899) was one of the best kings ever to rule mankind. He defended Anglo-Saxon England from Viking raids, formulated a code of laws, and fostered a rebirth of religious and scholarly activity. His reign exhibits military skill and innovation, sound governance and the ability to inspire men and plan for the future, piety and a practical commitment to the support of religion, personal scholarship and the promotion of education.

Lesson 4

Viking raids on England started in the late 8th century. The attack on Lindisfarne monastery in 793 was a particularly dramatic and significant event, heralding the onset of frequent raids on coastal communities, with churches and monasteries being particularly targeted for their wealth. Sporadic raiding gradually turned to larger scale assaults, as war-bands amalgamated, and these took on a more political aim. Over-wintering in defended camps, the control of extensive areas of land, and the extraction of "protection money" (the so-called Danegeld) became characteristic of Viking activity in England. But the Vikings were not colonizing England. Therefore, their numbers did not increase. Eventually, King Alfred of Wessex was able to confront the Viking "Great Army" at Edington, in 878, when his victory enabled him to establish terms for peace, though this did not put a complete stop to Viking activity, which continued on and off for several more generations. Alfred had to concede the northern and eastern counties to the Vikings, where their disbanded armies settled, created new settlements and merged with the local populations. While some Viking influences remain even today, they were essentially absorbed into the English population and disappeared as a distinctive group within two generations.

Chapter 4

Lesson 1

For the last time, a foreign power conquered England. Besides instituting a warrior culture, the Normal Conquest ushered in feudalism and chivalry, hallmarks of medieval Europe.

Lesson 2

In modern history, the German superiority in military

tactics and material enabled Germany, in World War II, to conquer most of Europe, with vastly inferior numbers. Likewise, American success in foreign wars, especially recently, has been partly tied to technological superiority over enemies.

Lesson 3

London was the first British city to recognize William the Conqueror's authority and this assured special status for London. This special status of London, which was answerable only to the king and enjoyed his full protection, was a strong influence in making it the outstanding commercial center. William made sure that London prospered and enjoyed several decades of peace.

Lesson 4

A. In epistemology (the study of knowledge) and in its modern sense, rationalism is any view appealing to reason as a source of knowledge or justification. In more technical terms, it is a method or a theory in which the criterion of the truth is not sensory but intellectual and deductive. The Christian faith, however, is part of phenomenology (the study of abstract truth). How does one rationally explain love? Hope? Truth? How does one use reason to explain how God could love an ungrateful, sinful race of man so much that He would send His only begotten Son to die for its sins?

B. Erasmus' views were very close to epicureanism. Epicureanism is a system of philosophy based upon the teachings of Epicurus. Epicurus believed that the greatest good was to seek modest pleasures in order to attain a state of tranquility and freedom from fear, as well as absence of bodily pain through knowledge of the workings of the world and the limits of one's desires. The combination of these two states is supposed to constitute happiness in its highest form. That sounds good. But the truth is Christians are called to obey God whether it is comfortable or not. Human happiness is secondary to God's purposes.

C. Bacon, who was a committed Christian, was flirting with some dangerous thoughts. First, it is doubtful that Bacon was using "salvation" the same way that theologians use the term. Bacon probably meant that scientific knowledge could lead to a better life. The danger is that Bacon's disciples might take him at his word and in fact believe that "scientific breakthroughs will lead to salvation."

D. Harold Kushner wrote a book with a similar title and he concluded that God is powerless to keep bad things from happening to good people. Indeed. The truth is, there are no "good" people—all have sinned and fallen short of the glory of God. Having said that, bad things to happen to redeemed innocent people. It is obvious that an explanation may not be forthcoming. Yet, these bad things are mitigated by the truth that everything that happens has a purpose; that all things that happen are meant to be good for the believer (Romans 8). This ontological fact blows up any anemic theory that paints a powerless God.

Chapter 5

Lesson 1

Henry VIII was a significant figure in the history of the English monarchy. Besides his six marriages, he was the cause of the separation of the Church of England from the Roman Catholic Church. Henry's struggles with Rome ultimately led to the separation of the Church of England from papal authority, the Dissolution of the Monasteries, and established himself as the Supreme Head of the Church of England. This was one of the first monarchies in Europe to do so. Never had a secular ruler claimed to be the head of religious institution. Henry also created the legal union of England and Wales with the Laws in Wales Acts 1535–1542.

Lesson 2

While the Church of England was separated from Rome in authority, its liturgy and theology were very similar. The real English Reformation would not occur until the Puritan Revolution in the next century.

Lesson 3

The weakening of the urban church, especially the African-American urban church, has had a devastating effect on this country. How? Urban flight and federal welfare have weakened the American urban church. Many capable and prosperous saints fled the city. At the same time, the federal government has created a nation of dependents who trust in Uncle Sam rather than God and His Church to meet their needs.

Lesson 4

This author shares More's belief that the church and state must never be separated. "I think that when statesmen forsake their own private conscience for the sake of their public duties, they lead their country by a short route to chaos." In America, for instance, Judeo-Christian values, so fervently embraced by the designers of the United States Constitution, are ignored at great peril.

Chapter 6

Lesson 1

A. Elizabeth understood and fervently sought public support for her person and policies. In that sense she was ambitious. She was a masterful campaigner and resourceful public relations expert. She embraced Parliament. Elizabeth worked hard and surrounded herself with capable counselors, counselors who were honest advisors, not sycophants. Her wise rule brought England out of the Middle Ages to the modern era. She was not a saint but she loved England and gave her nation her very best effort.

B. Answers will vary. In all due respect to John Knox, whom this author much admires, Queen Elizabeth was a capable monarch and seemed to be God's person for this time.

Lesson 2

The Spanish Armada was defeated by inept leadership, skillful British tactics, and horrendous weather. Spanish material was inferior. Exam-ination of Spanish cannon balls recovered from wrecks showed the Armada's ammunition to be badly cast, the iron lacking the correct composition and too brittle, causing the balls to disintegrate on impact, rather than penetrating the ship hulls. Several guns were found to have been badly cast and of inadequate composition, increasing the danger of bursting and killing or injuring the gun crews. A further important advantage for the English was the leadership of the sea captain over all on board his ship with a single clear chain of command. Spanish captains enjoyed no such authority. There was only one significant battle. On Monday, July 29, the two fleets met in battle off Gravelines. The English emerged victorious, although the Spanish losses were not great; only three ships were reported sunk, one captured, and four more ran aground. Nevertheless, the Spanish captain determined that the Armada must return to Spain. The English blocked the Channel, so the only route open was north around the tip of Scotland, and down the coast of Ireland. A succession of storms scattered the Spanish ships, resulting in heavy losses. By the time the tattered Armada regained Spain, it had lost half its ships and three-quarters of its men.

Lesson 3

By 1500, England was arguably the most politically and industrially advanced nation in Europe. Despite these advances, England had experienced a tumultuous recent past. The Hundred Years War with France (1337–1453) was both expensive and divisive. Natural disaster in the form of the Black Death (1348) took a tremendous toll and helped to weaken the feudal system, that ancient form of social organization in England. On top of that, England's early endeavors in the Western Hemisphere trailed those of Spain and France, and were generally unsuccessful. John Cabot was sent by Henry VII in 1497 search for the Northwest Passage to India. He cruised coastal Newfoundland and noted the excellent fishing opportunities along the Grand Banks, but he found no Northwest Passage. Even colonization initially failed. In the mid-1580s, Walter Raleigh sponsored attempts to establish a permanent colony in the area of Virginia; the famous effort on Roanoke Island — the famous "Lost Colony"—was part of that effort. Things would change, though, for several reasons.

- Hostility toward religious dissenters in England provoked many of them to embark on a perilous voyage and suffer hardship in a remote colony in exchange for the opportunity to worship as they believed. This drew thousands of talented, hardworking, and loyal British citizens to the New World. The British, ironically, then, colonized more of the New World, more quickly, than the Spanish, Dutch, or French.

- New forms of business organization developed, which provided sufficient funding for the establishment of colonies. Some of the new investors were content to wait a period of years for a return, rather than demand immediate profits from gold and silver. In other words, the British found a way to make money in the New World without finding a Northwest Passage or gold.

Lesson 4

Days out at the Globe Theatre would have been an exciting event. The grounds surrounding the Globe Theatre would have been full of people anxious to get the best location in the theater. There were no seats. Everyone stood. There would be vendors selling merchandise and souvenirs—no programs but yummy snacks like pickled pig's feet and chestnuts—creating a market day atmosphere. A trumpet was sounded to announce that the play was about to begin at the Globe Theatre in order for people to take their final places. Towering above the Globe was a small tower with a flag pole. Flags were used as a form of Elizabethan advertising! Flags were erected on the day of the performance which sometimes displayed a picture advertising the next play to be performed. Colour coding was also used—a black flag meant a tragedy, white a comedy and red a history. The Globe theatre allowed stage productions to become quite sophisticated with the use of massive props such as fully working cannons. Special effects were common. There were no female actresses—male actors, often young boys, played female parts. In just two weeks Elizabethan theatres could often present "eleven performances of ten different plays."

Chapter 7

Lesson 1

Answers will vary. Americans today regularly live into their 70s and generally women live longer than men. Hygiene and medicine have of course changed everything. Almost everything is different—housing, vocation, and military service.

Lesson 2

A. Mary Queen of Scots, only legitimate child of James V, was born in Scotland but spent most of her life in France, where she embraced Roman Catholicism and French manners. She was an extraordinarily beautiful and intelligent woman, but, ultimately the combination of French, Catholic, and cousin to Elizabeth, doomed her and she was beheaded by Elizabeth I.

B. Answers will vary, but this reader certainly would object. On the other hand, there is a pastor in Uganda, Africa, who has armed his elders with AK47s because his parishioners have been constantly murdered and harassed by violent revolutionaries. While this may be extreme, who can blame this pastor? This analogy, though, admittedly, is not the same as John Knox, who, while he was a sincere churchman was also a loyal Scottish patriot.

Lesson 3

A. At the heart of Hobbes' philosophy is the "struggle." It is in a struggle that truth emerges. Therefore, in pure Marxist theory, the proletariat—or workers—are in an epic struggle with the bourgeoisie —the owners. Ultimately, the workers will overcome the bourgeoisie and a sort of workers, utopia will result.

B. René Descartes is often credited with being the "Father of Modern Philosophy." This title is justified due to his break with the traditional Christian/scholastic philosophy prevalent at his time. Descartes attempted to address this via his method of doubt. His basic strategy was to consider false any belief that falls prey to even the slightest doubt. From here Descartes sets out to find something that lies beyond all doubt. He eventually discovers that "I exist" is impossible to doubt and is, therefore, absolutely certain. Now, however, reality moves away from God, and His Word, and resides in the human person where it remained in Western philosophy forever. Descartes became the father of the selfish reductionist nihilism that is postmodernism.

Lesson 4

Parliament, the legislative arm of Great Britain, developed naturally out of the daily political needs of the English king who had to deal with a participatory democracy. Parliament originated from two features of Anglo-Saxon government from the 8th to 11th centuries. These were the Witan and the Moot.

The Witan was a meeting where the king convened a meeting of his leading advisors and nobles to discuss matters affecting the country. It existed only when the king chose and was made up of those individuals whom he particularly summoned. Also, under the Anglo-Saxons there had been regular meetings, or moots, for each county (or shire) where local issues discussed. The local lords and bishops, and most importantly, four representatives of each village attended the "shire moot." After the Norman Conquest, this meeting became known as the County Court and it introduced the idea of representative government at the local level. These two gatherings remained separate for many centuries, but eventually the noble councilors of the Great Council and the local spokesmen of the County Court would combine to make a Parliament of two Houses, the aristocratic Lords and the locally representative Commons. With these representative bodies in place the implementation of the Magna Carta assured future Englishmen that they would have a representative democracy

Chapter 8

Lessson 1

The Elizabethan welfare system was not created to work with the numbers of poor, and degree of poverty that exists in contemporary America. Yet, in its own way, it was remarkably successful in its attempt to ameliorate the lives of thousands of poor. The welfare system today, too, creates dependency on the system in a way that Elizabethan intervention did not. Today, some poor people are able to obtain housing, food, and medical care without any effort on their part. Many sociologists claim that this creates "dependency" that, in the long run, takes power and initiative away from the ones whom it is meant to help.

Lesson 2

The only explanation is (1) Mrs. Peverell really was a witch, and under Elizabethan law, witchcraft was a capital offense. Mrs. Waterhouse was innocent. (2) Or there were mitigating circumstances. For example, perhaps Mrs. Waterhouse had irritated the court, or she was a strange, peculiar person. No one can know for sure. Were they punished appropriately? While the author does not support capital punishment for witchcraft, he does believe it existed in Elizabethan times (and today).

Lesson 3

Societies, including Elizabethan society, have tried a wide variety of programs dealing with specific medical problems and providing health care for certain groups. In America, the attempt to implement national health care started about 1912. The problem for Queen Elizabeth and the problem for contemporary Americans is twofold: How does a government control medical costs and how does a government ration health care? How does a government make decisions for individuals who may wish to receive elective procedures that are costly and the federal government deems unnecessary? Who makes the final decision?

Lesson 4

Elizabeth I was an innovative monarch who ruled well. Besides offering decades of peace (after defeating the Spanish Armada), Elizabeth encouraged innovative social welfare policy and medicinal interventions. She was a patron of the arts and encouraged men and women like William Shakespeare, Edmund Spenser, and Christopher Marlowe. Once serious economic issues were overcome, the Elizabethan area was a time of great prosperity.

Chapter 9

Lesson 1

James was an experienced monarch when he ascended the English throne, having been King of Scotland since his infancy. He received an education the equal of Elizabeth's and (in theory) developed a similarly balanced approach to governing. Like Elizabeth, James also had artistic aspirations. In theory, he was the perfect monarch to follow such a capable and colorful predecessor as Queen Elizabeth. But James I was not Elizabeth. Everything about James was "extravagant." On Elizabeth's death, England welcomed James and his royal family enthusiastically. People flocked to James on his way from Scotland, turning his southward journey into a grand procession. He immediately showed himself more liberal in his favors than Elizabeth, granting over 300 knighthoods before even reaching London. Likewise, James's extravagant lifestyle put huge strains on royal finances. He also showed intransigence toward religious toleration. In spite of King James' efforts, his reign more or less invited the English Civil War in a few short years.

Lesson 2

No. England was committed to a constitutional monarchy, where power lay in a constitution (e.g., Magna Carta), not in a body politic. Murdering Parliament would have unleashed momentary chaos, but ultimately the English people would not have tolerated mob rule.

Lesson 3

For the first time, residents had clean drinking water! At the same time, plagues killed thousands of people and a fire decimated the buildings. No doubt London smelled. The garbage was dumped into the streets, chamber pots were emptied out of the bedroom windows. People rarely bathed. Pigs ran through the streets eating the refuse. On the floor in houses or huts; rushes (cut reeds) were used as a covering instead of carpet, which had not reached England yet. The rushes in some homes were never changed and full of small rodents. The stocks often had someone who had committed a crime in full view of the public, to be mocked by them and have refuse thrown at them. London was noisy. Bells were used to advertise special goods. Church bells announced the time.

Lesson 4

The King James Bible, for its time, was the most readable, accurate Bible in the world. It was reasonably inexpensive and could be owned by almost any English family. King James wanted the Bible to be available to any Englishman who wanted it.

Chapter 10

Lesson 1

A. Charles presumed to manifest powers which compromised the Magna Carta. Also, in the early years of the English Civil War, the Scottish Presbyterians were Calvinists but they were not Puritans. They were allies in the English Civil War. This author believes that the Puritans and Scottish Presbyterians were sincere in their beliefs. In that sense, the English Civil War was a religious war—between the Church of England and dissenters. But, on another level, it was a struggle between the crown and Parliament. It was the last gasp of an English monarchy that sought to rule by divine right.

B. King Charles' demands were no more than Henry VIII had obtained. He was not bringing Catholicism back to England; he merely insisted on conformity to the English Church that the majority of his countrymen already embraced. From his perspective, the monarchy had lost too many rights over the years and an adjustment was in order.

Lesson 2

A. The Roundheads won the English Civil War because they had the most competent army. The Cavaliers could never sustain any string of military victories that would stop the Roundheads.

B. While this author would no doubt join the Parliamentarians, this does not mean that he supports their excesses, especially the execution of King Charles I.

Lesson 3

No, Perry is correct. The Puritan Divines were some of the most sincere, uncomplicated religious people in all of history. A cursory look at the works of John Milton, for instance, evidence a profound and abiding sincerity and depth of feeling toward God. These Christians did not merely talk the talk, they walked the walk!

Lesson 4

Paul reminds us in Romans 12 that Christian must not overcome evil with evil. Cromwell did go too far.

Chapter 11

Lesson 1

The Civil War, with all its excesses, was a step forward on the road to individual liberty/freedom. The conflict solidified Parliament as an influential institution in English politics. Charles I was the reactionary conservative who wanted to conserve and protect the status quo. Puritans were progressives who only wanted what was best for the masses. The religious element was terribly important. The Puritans were God-fearing, freedom-loving pragmatists who reluctantly rebelled against recalcitrant royalty. When freedom-loving Puritans could no longer live in a regime that Charles I oversaw, they rebelled.

Lesson 2

Parliament kept most common laws, but passed many restrictive 'moral' laws to regulate people's behavior, such as closing down theaters and requiring strict observance of the Sabbath. Ultimately they went too far and Cromwell felt compelled to dismiss them—just as Charles I did several years before. Cromwell believed in Parliamentary-led government; however, with foreign threats, the trouble in Ireland, and domestic squabbles, Cromwell felt that he could not govern through Parliament and he dismissed them.

Lesson 3

The primary reason was that the government used the joint stock company to fund exploration and colonization. A joint-stock company (JSC) is a partnership involving two or more legal persons. Certificates of ownership (or stocks) are issued by the company in return for each financial contribution, and the shareholders are free to transfer their ownership interest at any time by selling their stockholding to others.

Lesson 4

It was able to supply a very desirable, high quality, very profitably product(s) to a grateful, growing market, at an affordable price.

Chapter 12

Lesson 1

This reader disagrees with Belloc. There was a natural reaction to the staid world of the Puritans, but that hardly justified the hedonism that Charles II introduced to England. Also, Charles II was a hypocrite. While espousing religious freedom, what he was really trying to do was to return Roman Catholicism to the English monarchy. While this reader has no problem with Roman Catholicism, he does resent a monarch doing so under false pretences.

Lesson 2

It purged the city of the Great Plague that had already killed 20 percent of the population. It destroyed old, unsafe buildings and allowed the city fathers to undertake an ambitious building program of much more durable buildings.

Lesson 3

England was a much more advanced, industrial country than Ireland. It sought hegemony over the region because of abundant natural resources. Later, Ireland became a strategic possession to block Spanish expansion. Finally, when the English people settled in Ulster (Northern Ireland), England felt obligated to protect its own nationals.

Lesson 4

A. Spinoza argues, 'The perfection of things is to be reckoned only from their own nature and power; things are not more or less perfect, according as they delight or offend human senses, or according as they are serviceable or repugnant to mankind." Certainly Christians applaud Spinoza for embracing morality. However, one cannot base a moral/ethical code on human behavior or pleasure, as Spinoza does. Morality and ethics are based on external truths, based on the Word of God.

B. He regarded the mind of a person at birth as a tabula rasa—a blank slate upon which experience imprinted knowledge—and did not believe in the subjective. Locke believed in unalienable rights, rights that were given by God or another absolute power and were not given by government. If government did not give these rights, then it could not take them away. Inherent in Lockian thought was the notion that people were basically good. It followed, then, since people were basically good, the best government was government that governed the least. This reader is glad that our Founding Fathers were Lockian. The best government is the government that governs the least. But what is true in human government, is not true in moral government. People are not basically good—unredeemed people are lost in sin. The Kingdom of God is not a democracy. God is in control.

Chapter 13

Lesson 1

Seventeenth century Englishmen were acutely aware of the fact that they had certain natural rights, and rights of law, given to them by God, not by the king. Thus, they felt comfortable to assert those rights, in a bloodless way, when they felt threatened. This came by having a century of tradition—tradition that did not exist in France a century later when the bloody French Revolution occurred.

Lesson 2

- By raising and keeping a standing army within this kingdom in time of peace without the consent of Parliament and quartering soldiers contrary to the law. (Amendment II)

- By prosecutions in the Court of King's Bench for matters and causes cognizable only in Parliament; and by diverse other arbitrary and illegal courses. And whereas of late years, partial, corrupt, and unqualified persons have been returned and served on juries in trials, and particularly diverse jurors in trials for high treason, which were not freeholders. (Amendments' III & IV)

- Excessive bail hath been required of persons committed in criminal cases, to elude the benefit of laws made for the liberty of the subjects. And excessive fines have been imposed; and illegal and cruel punishments inflicted. And several grants and promises made of fines and forfeitures, before any conviction or judgment against the persons, upon whom the same were to be levied. (Amendment IV)

- The Declaration of Rights says nothing about freedom of religion or the right to bear arms.

Lesson 3

These women wonder why they are not afforded the same rights as other Englishmen. "Have we not an equal interest with the men of this Nation, in those liberties and securities contained in the Petition of Right, and the other good laws of the land? Are any of our lives, limbs, liberties or goods to be taken from us more than from men, but by due process of law and conviction of twelve sworn men of the neighborhood?"

Lesson 4

Answers will vary.

Chapter 14

Lesson 1

This is not good at any time, but it was particularly bad in 17th-century England. England was facing many serious problems that were being ignored. These problems included religious conflict; government conflict between the Crown and Parliament; escalating urban problems; growing conflict in the American colonies; problems with other European powers like Spain and France.

Lesson 2

Queen Anne was a skillful, capable ruler, whose integrity and honor were surpassed only by her political views.

Lesson 3

Homesick German King George's ignorance of the English language and customs made cabinet positions extremely important. George's frequent absences required the creation of the post of Prime Minister, the majority leader in the House of Commons who acted in the king's stead. The first was Robert Walpole. His success put him in the position of dominating British politics for the next 20 years, and the reliance on an executive Cabinet marked an important step in the formation of a modern constitutional monarchy in England.

Lesson 4

Penn was the only person who made major contributions to liberty in both the New World and the Old World. Before he conceived the idea of Pennsylvania, he became the leading defender of religious toleration in England. He was imprisoned six times for speaking out courageously. While in prison, he wrote one pamphlet after another, which gave Quakers a corpus of material to reference. He was fond of using the English courts to advance righteous causes—one of his cases helped secure the right to trial by jury. Penn used his diplomatic skills and family connections to save many Quakers from the gallows.

Chapter 15

Lesson 1

Answers will vary. The Whigs and Tories were the first political parties in world history. The Whigs historically wanted the Parliament, specifically the House of Commons, to be the strongest political entity. Whigs generally were anti-Catholic and anti-royalty. The other political group, the Court Party, were for the king and believed in Divine Rights. They were also in favor of the Church of England with all its ceremonies and episcopacy. The Whigs became the Liberal Party in the 19th century and the Tories became the Conservative Party. Both still exist today, although the Liberal Party is now called the Social Democratic Party.

Lesson 2

Historians argue that King George possessed three passions: the army, music and his wife. He was a courageous soldier and has the distinction of being the last British sovereign to command troops in the field. Caroline proved to be his greatest asset. She revived traditional court life, was fiercely intelligent and an ardent supporter of Robert Walpole. Walpole continued in the role of Prime Minister at Caroline's behest. Caroline's support of the Prime Minister was vital to the future of English history.

Lesson 3

While I would want to respect the office of king, and be careful to replace him, once his behavior harmed himself, and the state, I would vote to have him replaced in a quiet, humane way.

Lesson 4

Georgian London was experiencing urban growth in earnest. With the growth of the still nascent British Empire, London was becoming a more cosmopolitan nation. Stuart London, on the other hand, was more of a medieval village.

Chapter 16

Lesson 1

In the wake of the Glorious Revolution the fervent Catholic Louis XIV, the king of France, was not too pleased that pro-Catholic James II was replaced by two Protestants. Besides, he believed in the divine right to rule, like King James II, and didn't want English notions of democracy to spread to other parts of Europe.

As a result, war between the two nations followed. This war was reflected in America, as King William rejected an offer of colonial neutrality, and it is known as "King William's War." The war in Europe was about Roman Catholicism and French fears of English democracy gaining a foothold in formerly European bastions of monarchical despotism. In America, the war was between the French and the English over domination of the North American continent.

Lesson 2

A. Answers will vary, but in this case, Marlborough seemed to be the man for the age, a man who made great victories.

B. Nation states, particularly France and Russia, consolidated their power in the early modern period and they witnessed tragic economic dislocations, oppression, and wars leading to waves of terrorism and revolution that mirror our contemporary world situation in striking ways. Ethnic groups were "cleansed" (e.g., the Huguenots). Urban problems emerged in Paris, London, and Lisbon. In short, this age was very similar to our present age. Iraq and especially Iran emerged as modern nations by creating a straw man enemy to tear down and to blame for their problems.

Lesson 3

There was a feeling among European monarchs that they should block democratic impulses in their nascent stages. Furthermore, they sought to keep a balance of power where no one country was too powerful in Europe. England, in particular, with its domineering navy and growing empire was a great threat to much of Europe.

Lesson 4

A free press is indeed important to a free society; however, when the press sensationalizes political events, in a time of crisis, or misrepresents the facts in the same crisis, then the free press should be temporarily curbed.

Chapter 17

Lesson 1

At its peak, the British Empire was the largest empire that the world had ever known, much larger than the Roman Empire. The empire stretched all over the globe. Why were the British able to supplant the Portuguese, Dutch and Spanish Empires in the 17th and 18th centuries and effectively see off French, Russian and German challenges over the 19th and early 20th century? The British had "religious zeal" to spread their civilization. The Protestant aspect of Christianity was seen by many within the British Empire as part of the larger battle with the more Catholic nations of Continental Europe. Ever since the Reformation, religion represented not merely a spiritual difference between the Catholic and Protestant churches but was part of a far larger cultural and political competition between deadly rivals. Religion gave an excuse for this commercial rivalry to turn into military and political competition. The English planted their Protestant faith on foreign soils with as much fervency as the French and Spanish planted the Roman Catholic flag on theirs. Indeed, the so-called Protestant ethic—that hard work assured God's favor on an endeavor—assured British commercial success around the world. It was certainly helpful that the Protestant work ethic meant that Christian and commercial ideals could be reconciled fairly easily and in fact was thought to manifest itself in the improvement and development of British civilization in general. In pre-industrial Britain, the combination of these factors would lead to the creation of successful colonies in North America.

Lesson 2

Mercantilism and Chartered Monopoly Companies were successful British models employed to expand the Empire. The king or queen would give permission, or a chartered monopoly, to explorers to claim lands on his behalf and then authorize certain companies to exploit the natural resources in that part of the world in return for a fixed income to the Monarch. In many ways it was something for nothing for the ruler. These companies would buy the privilege to have a monopoly. For instance, the East India Trading Company had a monopoly on tea trade from India. Besides paying the monarchy a yearly retainer, the East India Company promised to keep prices reasonable. The Spanish and Portuguese used this first, and the French and Dutch followed suit. It brought great profits to companies and to the nation.

Combined with the lucrative practice of mercantilism was the British penchant to embrace innovation and technology. British weaponry was very effective and its communication systems allowed it to govern its far flung empire. Its combination of industrial might and maritime power meant that it had a peculiar advantage

Lesson 3

Nations must be careful to keep the national interests of

the state before the interests of the company. Likewise, moral issues must be paramount too. Slavery, for instance, no matter how profitable, must not be allowed.

Lesson 4

The American colonies had substantial advantages. For one thing, they were defending their homeland; the British were enforcing their national will. The American nation was huge and a long way from England. Essentially, all America had to do was to hold out until Great Britain grew too tired to fight. For the British, the theater of the war offered many problems. From first to last it extended from Massachusetts to Georgia, a distance of almost a thousand miles. It was nearly three thousand miles from the main base of supplies and, though the British navy kept the channel open, transports were constantly falling prey to daring privateers and fleet American war vessels. The sea, on the other hand, offered an easy means of transportation between points along the coast and gave ready access to the American centers of wealth and population. Of this the British made good use. Though early forced to give up Boston, they seized New York and kept it until the end of the war; they took Philadelphia and retained it until threatened by the approach of the French fleet; and they captured and held both Savannah and Charleston. Wars, however, are seldom won by the conquest of cities. America was a land of rural farms and small towns–it was not dependent upon its urban centers (Beard). Finally, if disorganized, the Americans were natural soldiers and showed ingenuity and poise in the face of adversity. Given time, the Americans would win. General George Washington knew it. A mediocre general at best, George Washington managed to lose virtually every battle he fought, but he won the war! Washington knew that eventually the British would grow tired and abandon their efforts to subjugate the colonists. The British were in fact battered and worn down by a guerrilla war and outdone on two important occasions by superior forces—at Saratoga and Yorktown. Like America learned in Vietnam and Iraq, the British understood that an immense army, which could be raised only by a supreme effort, would be necessary to subdue the colonies and there was doubt anything would work. To the British, the American colonies just were not worth it. Cornwallis surrendered at Yorktown, Virginia, in 1781 and the military phase of the war was over.

Chapter 18

Lesson 1

The French Revolution and romanticism rejected the Age of Enlightenment. Romanticism's response to the French Revolution is significant because it posed a stark and purposeful contrast to the attitudes that defined the Age of Enlightenment. The Enlightenment focused more on reason and rationality as the voice of authority and used science and logic to explain nature. Romanticism, on the other hand, focused more on the individual as opposed to the state and emotion above reason. The visual art and literature that came from romanticism elevated nature to a metaphysical, ubiquitous status. Also, romanticism typically celebrated the middle class as the conduit of truth and goodness. Ordinary people were unshackled from the pretentious superficiality of the cultured, educated, upper class.

Lesson 2

In both America, and in Britain, freedom-loving citizens paused to consider what can happen when a nation embraces "liberty, equality, and fraternity" without a concomitant commitment to compromise, justice, mercy, and candor. The French Revolution, the most egalitarian of revolutions, ended in wanton, gratuitous bloodshed that more or less closed the book on fundamental rights for all time.

Lesson 3

Both articles are full of prejudicial material. Here is one example: The Goths and Vandals, when they levelled the gates of Rome, and triumphantly entered into the capitol, yet still retained those feelings which distinguished the mind of man from the ungovernable appetite of the brute creation. It is true, they commanded the Roman ladies to attend them with wine under the Plantain Trees, and insisted on the solders acting as slaves—but they neither violated the chastity of the one, nor deprived the others of life. Far otherwise has been the conduct of the French barbarians. They delight in that kind of murder, which is attended with cruelty, and rejoice in every occurrence which can debase and unsex the feelings of man.

- The French Revolutionaries are compared to barbarians, the Goths and Vandals.

- But they were worse than these barbarians!

- They violate the honor of women.

- The article uses inflammatory words like "murder"

and "debase" and "cruelty."

Lesson 4

Carlyle's history introduced English-speaking people to the full tragedy of the French Revolution. Carlyle does this by careful attention to facts and details, combined with his narrative style. Carlyle's history is more a story than history. In particular, he gives colorful characterizations of Louis XVI, Marie Antoinette, and Robespierre. Narrative history always has a danger of appearing trite or too familiar. The truth is Robespierre was one of kind. Let's hope the reader does not relate to him at all! On the other hand, narrative history is very readable and draws even the most reluctant reader into the maelstrom that was the French Revolution. It can also be sensational. English audiences were fascinated with Carlyle' gruesome details.

Chapter 19

Lesson 1

Godwin believed that people could be perfect, were in fact perfect. He believed that there were no innate principles, and therefore no original propensity to evil. Godwin argued "our virtues and our vices may be traced to the incidents which make the history of our lives, and if these incidents could be divested of every improper tendency, vice would be extirpated from the world." All control of man by man was more or less intolerable, and the day would come when each man, doing what seems right in his own eyes, would also be doing what is in fact best for the community, because all will be guided by principles of pure reason. "Morality is nothing else but that system which teaches us to contribute, upon all occasions, to the extent our power, to the well-being and happiness of every intellectual and sensitive existence. But there is no action of our lives, which does not in some way affect that happiness. Our property, our time, and our faculties, may all of them be made to contribute to this end. The periods, which cannot be spent in the active production of happiness, may be spent in preparation. There is not one of our avocations or amusements, that does not, by its effects, render us more or less fit to contribute our quota to the general utility. If then every one of our actions fall within the province of morals, it follows that we have no rights in relation to the selecting them. No one will maintain, that we have a right to trespass upon the dictates of morality." To a Christian, morality is based upon the Word of God. While there is some wiggle room concerning some moral positions, if humankind wishes to maintain a healthy life, it must adhere to biblical morality. If not, not only does the individual suffer, human society in general is damaged. Next, all have sinned and fallen short of the Kingdom of God. There is no one who is good separate from the redemptive power of the Cross. Finally, governments and authorities were established by God (Romans 14) and necessitate submission. Auth-ority is very good for the overall health of human society.

Lesson 2

How does one maintain liberty and equality at the same time? Will my liberty violate your equality?

Lesson 3

Parliament is the most powerful arm of British government. Government exists to protect and to serve the people, but, if necessary, to hold the people to higher standards than they would wish. Compromise is laudable and necessary in a democratic republic.

Lesson 4

A. Paine argues, "In the early ages of the world, according to the scripture chronology, there were no kings; the consequences of which was there were no wars; it is the pride of kings which throws mankind into confusion . . . The Heathens paid divine honors to their deceased kings, and the Christian world hath improved on the plan by doing the same to their living ones. How impious is the title of sacred majesty applied to a worm, who in the midst of his splendor is crumbling into dust. As the exalting one man so greatly above the rest cannot be justified on the equal rights of nature, so neither can it be defended on the authority of scripture; for the will of the Almighty, as declared by Gideon and the prophet Samuel, expressly disapproves of government by kings." Paine suggests that Israel's decision to choose a king (i.e., Saul) was not God's perfect plan—which is true. However, Paine forgot that God did not want Israel to establish a republic—He wished for them to be in an autocracy—with God Himself as the benevolent despot!

B. Paine begins this section by making a distinction between society and government. Paine then goes on to consider the relationship between government and society in a state of "natural liberty." Paine criticizes the English constitution by examining the relationship between the king, the peers, and the commons. Burke argues, "All government, indeed every human benefit and enjoyment, every virtue, and every prudent act, is founded on compromise and barter we give and take; we remit some rights, that we may enjoy others." People should invite different social classes, different races, into government because they will engender compromise which insures liberty for all. "Natural liberty," to Burke, is a euphemism describing nihilism, and chaos, that emerged in the Reign of Terror. Both agree that there are basic liberties that humankind shares; they disagree as to how these liberties are maintained.

Chapter 20

Lesson 1

A. Answers will vary. It is this author's opinion that Napoleon created the age, rather than vice versa. At just 30 years of age, Napoleon Bonaparte ruled the most powerful country in Europe. But the journey that led him there was neither inevitable nor smooth. Napoleon was a ruthless, ambitious, driven man whose character has been disguised by the public image he carefully fashioned to suit the purposes of his ambition. He was the first modern leader to be a master of "spin." He used the media to project an idealized image of himself.

B. The term Levée en masse was a draft of all able-bodied men to defend the nation and was an outgrowth of the political events in revolutionary France, namely the new concept of the democratic citizen as opposed to a royal subject. Since the nation now understood itself as a community of all people, its defense also was the responsibility of all. Thus, the Levée en masse was a means to defend the nation for the nation by the nation. Historically, the Levée en masse introduced the concept of the people's war and displaced prior restricted forms of warfare when armies of professional soldiers fought without general participation of the population.

Lesson 2

If ever there a country, whose future was determined by its army, it was the Napoleonic Wars. Napoleon and his army were the dominant players of the Napoleonic Wars. French national influence rose quickly with the Army and collapsed just as quickly after the disastrous invasion of Russia (1812). As one historian explains, "Napoleon and his famous Grande Armee reshaped both Europe and the art of war. Swift marching, furious in the attack, grimly enduring, high-hearted, stubborn in disaster, it still ranks among the few greatest of the great. It also was many men of many different nations - many heroes, not

a few cowards, and the multitude who were neither but did their duty as they saw it." Probably no army has fought such a variety of enemies in so short a space of time as did the French soldiers under Napoleon Bonaparte.

Lesson 3

A. In 1812, Napoleon enters Russia at the head of the largest army in world history. Backed by half a million soldiers, and with all of continental Europe under his command, he marches to Moscow. But nothing goes according to plan. Raging fire destroys Moscow. Ice and snow engulf the Grande Armee. While Napoleon was victorious over the Russian army, the Russian winter destroyed him. He allowed himself to be drawn too far away from his supply base and to forget that one should never conquer what one cannot hold!

B. In retrospect, Napoleon had virtually no chance to win. This was not 1807. France was staggering under 20 years of English blockades and huge war casualties. England and Prussia were flush with new vigor and spirit. Napoleon did not need a Valmey-like stalemate; he must have a stunning victory. England, on the other hand, only need to checkmate Napoleon. The outcome at Waterloo was a forgone conclusion.

Lesson 4

This is a story told to a group of peasants by an ex-soldier who served under Napoleon in almost all his campaigns. His audience are uneducated peasants. De Balzac is taking a stab at humor. Having an uncouth, uneducated audience, gives him a reason to present a similar rendition of history. The speaker is a "Huck Finn" character, loveable, insightful, even astute but also profane and humorous. Using an ordinary, but heroic speaker, and doing so to an unpretentious audience, disarms the reader and gives De Balzac opportunities to develop more personal, even controversial aspects of Napoleon's life.

Chapter 21

Lesson 1

The Industrial Revolution began in the 18th century. It was a time when major advances in agriculture, manufacturing, mining, and transport significantly affected life in England, then subsequently spreading throughout Europe, North America, and eventually the world. The onset of the Industrial Revolution marked a major turning point in human history; almost every aspect of daily life was eventually influenced in some way. Advances occurred in almost every industry: notably in textile and pottery manufacturing.

Lesson 2

Ultimately industrialization isolated family members and made family maintenance difficult. Later, in the 20th century, with the advent of television, this became even more difficult to maintain. Family members spent long hours separated from one another. The father worked in the coal mine. The mother worked in a textile mill. The daughters might be boarding in a far away city and working in a pottery mill. The boys might be doing piece work at another factory. Unfortunately, family members might not see each other but for a few hours each Sunday.

Lesson 3

A. Answers will vary.

B. Answers will vary. Clearly Wilberforce was a gradualist. Also, Christians must remember that the mean never justifies the end. One never overcomes evil with evil (Romans 12).

Lesson 4

Until this time, wealth was concentrated in the hands of a landed aristocracy. Now a new commercial class was emerging that controlled the majority of wealth.

Chapter 22

Lesson 1

A. One would hope, but, in fact, George IV did not violate any British laws.

B. There is, as one historian explains, a death of outrage. The general populace is invited to be irresponsible and immoral.

Lesson 2

British citizens knew full well that there was a rule of law that even kings had to abide. There were legitimate legislative avenues for the British to pursue to advance their causes without resorting to violence.

Lesson 3

It is unfortunate that young people would have to work for such low wages in such distressed conditions.

Lesson 4

The author feels that England was wrong to export grain from starving Ireland without making an allowance to provide for her people. If England took the domestic food supply it should be willing to provide a substitute, or pay the Irish fair compensation so that an alternative (e.g., wheat) might be imported from another country (e.g., USA).

Chapter 23

Lesson 1

Answers will vary. In the early part of the 21st century America is the most powerful nation on earth. Like Victorian England, the sun never sets on the American Empire. At the same time there are significant social problems at home and wars abroad. Time is going quickly but slowly at the same time!

Lesson 2

Civil disobedience is the active refusal to obey certain laws, demands, and commands of a government, or of an occupying international power. Civil disobedience is usually, but not always, defined as being nonviolent resistance. In its most nonviolent form it could be said that it is compassion in the form of respectful disagreement. Civil disobedience was very effective in Dr. Martin Luther King Jr.'s Civil Rights marches. When is it justified? When the cause is in line with Judeo-Christian values and is non-violent. Civil disobedience will only be effective when it is done in public.

Lesson 3

Sociologists took Darwinism and created a social theory of "survival of the fittest." This notion encourag social planners to ignore the poor and infirmed because society would not improve until the "weak" naturally died away. Science cannot easily be applied to social theory. Darwinism, as implausible as it may be in the scientific field, created havoc in sociology. Likewise, the theory of relativity is a far cry from the moral ethical idea of situational ethics (the notion that morality is based on circumstances rather than a moral code).

Lesson 4

Answers will vary. Weber is too sanguine about Protestantism—this author puts more stock in the English democratic tradition than he does in Protestantism

Chapter 24

Lesson 1

The gates of hell shall not prevail against the Church, but, in this era, as all modern eras, the Church and its confessions are under constant attack. The rise of secularism (the concept that government or other entities should exist separately from religion) is an inexorable move in history and Christians need to be vigilant to counteract its impact.

Lesson 2

Answers will vary. Eventually England will lose hegemony at the end of World War II, and this will doom England's empire.

Lesson 3

By the end of the 19th century, the Salvation Army was the primary social welfare agency to the entire city of London. In other words, no secular social welfare organization could hold a candle to the expertise and effectiveness of the Salvation Army. It was not merely a vital, effective evangelistic ministry; it was also the most effective social welfare organization in the 19th century. More poverty-stricken Londoners were helped by the Salvation Army than any other organization. And wherever the Salvation Army went, the Gospel of Jesus Christ was present.

Lesson 4

Florence Nightingale was a gifted, English nurse and orator. A Universalist, Nightingale believed that God had called her to be a nurse. She came to prominence for her pioneering work in nursing during the Crimean War, where she tended to wounded soldiers. Pankhurst's voice was "shrill and demanding." Nightingale's quiet, unassuming competence in some ways was more persuasive that women should have equal rights to men.

Chapter 25

Lesson 1

Nation building is a process of creating a new government in an unrelated nation. Usually this is accomplished primarily through the military. It rarely works unless the populace wish to participate in such a process.

Lesson 2

To check Russian ambitions to expand its empire to the Black, Caspian, and ultimately to the Med-iterranean Sea.

Lesson 3

Indian nationalists wished to have the British leave India. The Indian Mutiny erupted in May 1857, when loyal Indian troops massacred all the British in Delhi. The British eventually ended the mutiny, resorting to draconian tactics. The large city of Delhi was left in ruins.

Lesson 4

Probably not. While the advance of the Gospel is important, it does not necessarily have to follow political or military occupation.

Chapter 26

Lesson 1

The Portuguese were the first Europeans in West Africa. After the Portuguese open up the African coast to trade, in the 15th century, the other European nations of the Atlantic coast are soon sending their ships into the region. The first motive was piracy. As on the Spanish Main in America, ships returning to Europe laden with booty are attractive prey. The second lure was slave trading, which historically was immensely profitable, if also inhumane. Increasingly British privateers plundered Portuguese vessels but to win a share in the rich trade which the Portuguese pioneered—in gold, ivory, gum and above all slaves. To do this, England had to build their own fortified trading stations, or to seize such places already established by rivals. This England did. The story of British involvement in West Africa, from the Senegal River down to the Cape of Good Hope, was initially one of small markets along the coast often changing hands among European nations. The only settlement of any real permanency, and the only one where the settlers penetrate any distance inland, was the Dutch colony at the Cape of Good Hope, which later became South Africa.

Lesson 2

A. Livingston could and should have been more solicitous to his family. His children hardly knew him and he was away when his wife died in 1862. He could have taken them to Africa with him but this was something that apparently did not occur to him.

B. This question would have seemed irrelevant to Livingston, because basically they were one in the same. Presumably, though, Livingston would have chosen the

Kingdom of God above all.

Lesson 3

In December 1878, following the death of several British citizens at the hands of the Zulus, British authorities in South Africa issued an ultimatum to the Zulu king demanding that the perpetrators be turned over for trial. This request was refused and the British began preparations to invade Zululand. At first the British forces were defeated. However, the British inevitably held technological advantages that ultimately outweighed other disadvantages that ultimately gave the British victory.

Lesson 4

It was a matter of prestige and honor. Also, the English had tangential friends who were commercially valuable and they were looking at the British and wondering how they would fare in a similar situation. If the British lost face in Uganda, with marginal commercial interest, would unfriendly forces in South Africa be encouraged to stage a similar revolt?

Chapter 27

Lesson 1

Not only were the Boers fierce fighters, they had the advantage of fighting in an interior line (within territory in which they were familiar). They were also fighting for their homes and families. The Boer Wars were unconventional wars, wars for which the British were ill equipped to conduct.

Lesson 2

The Boxer Rebellion, also called The Boxer Uprising, by some historians or the Righteous Harmony Society Movement in northern China, was an anti-colonialist, anti-Christian movement by the "Righteous Harmony Society" or Boxers in China between 1898 and 1901. The uprising took place in response to imperialist expansion involving European opium traders, political invasion, economic manipulation, and missionary evangelism.

Lesson 3

The nature of the monarchy evolved through the influence of George V. In contrast to his grandmother and father—Victoria's ambition to exert political influence in the tradition of Elizabeth I's and Edward VII's aspirations to manipulate the destiny of nations—George's royal perspective was considerably less ambitious. As one historian explained, he was exactly like most of his subjects. He discovered a new job for modern kings and queens to do: representation.

Lesson 4

Answers will vary. Perhaps the computer or iPod would define our nation more than any other item.

Chapter 28

Lesson 1

Socialism—a theory of government that posited that the state should be a ubiquitous presence in the life of its people—grew in popularity. In the 20th century socialism became a powerful movement. Socialists believed the state should own industry and land. They also believed in economic equality. Wealth should be distributed to give everyone an equal share. However in the end socialism proved to be a failure. The redistribution of wealth never happened and in the late 20th century state owned industries were privatized. Socialism, though, discourages competition and initiative that inevitably creates shortages and shoddy workmanship.

Lesson 2

The following is a portion of an article that the author wrote for a magazine: In 49 B.C., the crossing of a small stream in northern Italy by ambitious Roman general Julius Caesar became one of the pivotal events in world history. From it sprang the Roman Empire and the genesis of modern Europe. An ancient Roman law forbade any general from crossing the Rubicon River and entering Italy proper with a standing army. To do so was treason. Caesar was well aware of this. Coming up with his troops on the banks of the Rubicon, he halted, and reminded his fellow officers of the importance of the next step. "Still we can retreat!" he said. "But once let us pass this little bridge, - and nothing is left but to fight it out with arms!" (Suetonius). He crossed the river and we all know the rest. America is very different from the America in which Karen and I began home schooling in 1985. Really different. Moral boundaries are violated; sacred fences are down. The first strophe of William Butler Yeats' poem "The Second Coming" begins:

> *Turning and turning in the widening gyre,*
> *The falcon cannot hear the falconer.*
> *fall apart; the centre cannot hold;*

Mere anarchy is loosed upon the world.
The blood-dimmed tide is tossed, and everywhere
The ceremony of innocence is drowned;
The best lack all conviction, while the worst
Are full of passionate intensity.

American in the beginning of the 21st century is spinning out of control. We are stretching our wings adventurously, but drifting farther away from our God. We are in trouble. In 1 Kings 18–19, Elijah and his peers live in a similar world. Choleric Elijah is coming home—and no one wants him to come home. He is crossing his Rubicon. After a long time, in the third year, the word of the LORD came to Elijah: "Go and present yourself to Ahab, and I will send rain on the land." King Ahab and Queen Jezebel, of course, hate him. But even, Obadiah, a faithful follower of God and trusted advisor to the king and queen, who had learned so well to survive in this hostile land, who has done so much good for God's people—Obadiah was not too thrilled to see him either. In fact, no one welcomed Elijah— not the hostile king and queen nor the pious evangelical Obadiah. Even though Elijah brings good news—it is finally going to rain—no one welcomes him. Elijah's fish-or-cut-bait prophetic messages are irritating the life out of the status quo. That is bad enough. But what really scares the dickens out of everyone is the fact that Elijah has come home to Zion, to the City of God, to challenge the gods of the age to a duel. There is nothing wrong with being Obadiah. Faithful, godly Obadiah, like Daniel, was very influential in a very evil regime. Obadiah served evil Ahab and Jezebel well, and he served God's people well too. For instance, he was able to protect hundreds of prophets who otherwise would have been killed by Ahab. King Ahab and Jezebel are very capable, and in many ways, successful monarchs. From their perspective, they are the true leaders. Elijah, and the prophets, is radical, unreasonable, uncompromising troublers of Israel. They are not team players. No doubt Ahab and Jezebel could not understand why Elijah could not carry on a civil discussion about what they saw as tangential, civil issues. Likewise, recently our president was genuinely concerned that "conservatives cannot be civil and polite in their discussions about abortion." To many of us pro-lifers, and to Elijah, murder and apostasy do not engender etiquette. Ahab and Jezebel are postmodernists. They celebrate the subjective. They are committed to compromise is their religion. Live and let live! What is the big deal? Well, you see, Elijah cannot compromise with the stuff they are doing. There is no wiggle room in Judah and there is getting to be precious little wiggle room in the USA too. There is some good news here. The world of the Baals, folks, is falling apart, and quickly. As sociologist Peter Berger explains, "American mainline culture can no longer offer plausibility structures for the common man. It no longer sustains Americans." Or, as my old friend Professor Harvey Cox, at Harvard, coyly observed, "Once Americans had dreams and no technology to fulfill those dreams. Now Americans have tons of technology, but they have no dreams left." In short order the Ahabs and Jezebels are going to find out that Elijah is not in a compromising mood either. Folks, there are some things one cannot compromise. Elijah and Jezebel are going to meet a man of God who speaks with concrete clarity, who carries the weight of truth. The days of Obadiah are over. Elijah is coming to town. This is the generation of Elijah. The generation that will have to walk the long, arduous walk up Mt. Carmel and they will challenge the gods of this age. Bring it on! We are ready! Every knee shall bow, every tongue shall profess, that Jesus Christ is Lord. Bring on the fire of Elijah, again, on this nation! God is calling forth our children—Elijahs who will go to the high places of our nation to challenge the prophets of Baal—in the courts, in the university, in the shop, in the home, in churches.

Lesson 3

In fact, much of what Nietzsche said is accurate. "God is dead," at least the "god" that the modernists and secularists created. But the God of the Old and New Testament is very much alive! Religion that has become a weak reflection of culture is also useless. But a religion that is life-changing and iconoclastic is life-giving. The former is the God the author serves and follows.

Lesson 4

The allure of science solving all modern problems is irresistible. But the realistic notion that there are consequences is equally unavoidable. Like Victor Frankenstein, some modernists have created "Frankenstein," which seemed like a good idea, only to discover that they had created a monster. For instance, advances in medical science have brought longer lives and prosperity to billions of people. But, at the same time, medical science murders 3,000 unborn American babies every day. It is on that horn of a dilemma that Shelley leaves her readers.

Chapter 29

Lesson 1

The biggest problem was Franz Joseph of the Austro-Hungarian Empire. It was a decadent empire full of malcontents. His army was mediocre; his civil service ineffectual. Franz Joseph started ruling in 1848, before the American Civil War. He was not prepared for the technological advances of the 20th century. In fact, he was hardly ready for anything that was emerging after 1900. Nonetheless, he alienated ethic minorities and more or less, through alliances, let Europe into World War I. Finally, Franz Joseph sent an army of 200,000 men into Bosnia. Franz Joseph had also stirred a hornet's nest that would one day send out millions of hornets who would sting him to death

Lesson 2

Even the most insignificant conflagrant activity, much less the assassination of a king, would lead to warfare between the most unimportant B countries, and, then, between their allies.

Lesson 3

The ocean was the life blood of England. Britain must have naval superiority.

Lesson 4

Humanity must not be surprised at the depth of human depravity. This is not to say that humankind is not capable of kindness and goodness. However, without proper limits, freedom can lead to horrible bloodshed.

Chapter 30

Lesson 1

World War I brought modernity that was characterized by highly industrialized states divided into social classes based on economic status. Modernity included regular pattern of everyday life, urbanization, influx of women at all levels of employment and business, secular outlook, sexual freedom, sharp reduction in birth rate and death rate, centralized bureaucratic government, standardized education system, and pervasive use of technology specially in communications.

Lesson 2

As a consequence of the lack of surprise generated by the advance bombardment, and the lack of success in cutting the German barbed wire and in damaging their underground bunkers, the BEF made strikingly little progress on July 1 or in the days and weeks that followed. The British troops were for the most part forced back into their trenches by the effectiveness of the German machine gun response. But there were some hopeful signs. The British used tanks for the first time. While they had great shock value, their strategic value was limited. Despite the slow but progressive British advance, poor weather—snow—brought a halt to the Somme offensive on November 18. During the attack the British and French had gained about 12 miles of ground, the taking of which resulted in 420,000 estimated British casualties, including many of the volunteer "pal's" battalions, plus a further 200,000 French casualties. German casualties were estimated at 500,000. Nonetheless, the British felt obligated to continue this carnage for almost 6 months. It was hoped that the great breakthrough would occur the next day.

Lesson 3

No doubt it was due to the fact that the Industrial Revolution had begun in England.

Lesson 4

Churchill showed early talent in journalism, writing, politics, and warfare. He truly was a genius. Sir Winston Leonard Spencer-Churchill was educated at Harrow and the Royal Military College at Sandhurst, and was sent to India with a cavalry commission in 1895. He won early fame as a war correspondent, covering the Cuban revolt against Spain (1895), and campaigns in the Northwest Frontier of India (1897), the Sudan (1898) and South Africa during the Boer War (1899). Churchill had authored five books by the age of 26. His escape from a Boer prison camp in 1899 made him a national hero and ushered him into the House of Commons, where his career spanned 60 years. So, it seems Churchill could do almost anything he liked!

Chapter 31

Lesson 1

A. First, territory was taken from Germany and her allies and given to the victors. Germany lost all her overseas colonies. Second, Germany's army was reduced to 100,000 men and not allowed to build tanks. Germany could have no air force. Next, she was allowed only 6 capital naval ships and no aircraft carriers. Huge reparations, or financial payments, were required of Germany.

Germany must pay for the war. Finally, a League of Nations was set up to keep world peace.

B. No one liked the Treaty of Versailles. The British public felt it was too soft. Germany thought it was too harsh. America rejected it altogether.

Lesson 2

To the British, the Great War (World War I) was a war to end all wars. Most soldiers, however, did not fight for a "cause." They fought to protect their "pals."

Lesson 3

By most estimates, the influenza pandemic of 1918–1919 killed more people than World War I. It killed between 20 and 40 million people. It has been cited as the most devastating epidemic in recorded world history. More people died of influenza in a single year than in four-years of the Black Death Bubonic Plague from 1347 to 1351. World War I brought together thousands of soldiers who spread the disease.

Lesson 4

While its physical structures were basically intact, like so many English towns, its people were broken. Whole sections of the city's young men had been sacificed on the Somme. The ones who were left were further decimated by the flu expidemic. London was full of sadness. Yet, it was a staid, proud English city. It was the victor, after all, and this no doubt brought business to the small shops along the Thames. In the next decade London was to know unprecedented prosperity.

Chapter 32

Lesson 1

England lost both its political and its economic hegemony. The cost of the war was so great that England consumed all of its credits and became heavily indebted to the United States. As a result of the war, the world's financial center shifted from England to the United States, from London to New York. In France, the heavy losses in manpower at the front decimated an entire generation of Frenchmen and created a serious leadership vacuum. France also suffered untold property damage since most of the war on the Western Front was fought on French soil. Germany had entered World War I as the greatest power among the belligerents, with its people immensely proud of Germany's achievements in the years since unification. Defeat in war was a profound

shock, and coupled with economic privation and collapse, was disillusioning. Severe economic difficulties created by the war and the demand for reparations caused despair and hardship that ensured an uncertain future for the nation.

In other words, the war accelerated the process of change driven by industrialization, and created circumstances in Germany, in the Balkans, and in Russia, which people were not prepared for. As previously indicated, it also thrust the United States into a position of world leadership before the American people were ready to accept that responsibility. The problems, the instability, the uncertainties, and the economic collapse created by the war were far more difficult to deal with than any situation that had existed prior to the war (from the student edition).

Lesson 2

In the years immediately after the First World War, the "War to End All Wars," a promising new era of democracy emerged. The despotic monarchies in Russia, Germany and Austria, were all overthrown and replaced by representative democracies or socialist states. Democracy seemed to have triumphed over autocracy. Yet within two decades, by 1928, some sort of dictatorship replaced most European countries. Russia was the worst. Italy was the first. And Germany had the most capable dictator. Similar dictatorships emerged in the Balkan countries. Only Britain and France remained democratic. What was the allure? Ironically, totalitarian states were more prosperous during the Depression (1928–1940) than democratic states. The centrally controlled economy enabled the totalitarian dictatorship to exploit its population. During this era dictators kept their economies stimulated through preparation for war.

Lesson 3

Initially, England, who historically loved a stable Europe, welcomed a Nazi Germany. The Weimar Republic was far too unstable. A stable Germany meant a stable Europe. A stable Europe was good for business. More importantly, a powerful Ger-many was a desirable buffer with Communist Russia. To the British, the Soviet communist threat was much greater than the German threat. In general though, concerning Germany, most English citizens simply could not believe that Adolf Hitler was as evil as he appeared. He was an anamoly. England tried to treat him like any reasonable European statesman. But Hitler was not a normal European statesmen. Even a cursory reading of *Mein Kamf* would evidence that fact, but, apparently England did not want to think about it. This was a time when the children, many of them orphans, were reaching adulthood. World War I was still a terrible memory and they certainly did not want to repeat the same mistakes as their fathers had made. Hitler, then, was tolerated, even admired, by many English.

Lesson 4

Japanese pan-Asian views, and growing industrial and military might, spelled the end of British predominance in the Pacific Rim.

Chapter 33

Lesson 1

There was first, Old England, the country of the cathedrals and minsters and manor houses and inns, of parson and Squire; guide-book and quaint highways and byways England . . . Then, I decided, there is the nineteenth-century England, the industrial England of coal, iron, steel, cotton, wool, railways; of thousands of rows of little houses all alike, sham Gothic churches, square-faced chapels, Town Halls, Mechanics' Institutes, mills, foundries, warehouses, refined watering-places, Pier Pavilions, Family and Commercial Hotels, Literary and Philosophical Societies, back-to-back houses, detached villas with monkey-trees, Grill Rooms, railway stations, slag-heaps and 'tips', dock roads, Refreshment Rooms, doss-houses, Unionist or Liberal Clubs, cindery waste ground, mill chimneys, slums, fried-fish shops, public-houses with red blinds, bethels in corrugated iron, good-class draper's and confectioners' shops, a cynically devastated countryside, sooty dismal little towns, and still sootier grim fortress-like cities. This England makes up the larger part of the Midlands and the North and exists everywhere; but it is not been added to and has no new life poured into it. . . The third England, I concluded, was the new post-war England, belonging far more to the age itself than to this particular island. America, I supposed, was its real birthplace. This is the England of arterial and by-pass roads, of filling stations and factories that look like exhibition buildings, of giant cinemas and dance-halls and cafes, bungalows with tiny garages, cocktail bars, Woolworths, motor-coaches, wireless, hiking, factory girls looking like actresses, greyhound racing and dirt tracks, swimming pools, and everything given away for cigarette coupons.

Lesson 2

Henry VIII was a capable, but immoral, colorful king who instigated the English Reformation. Queen Elizabeth I was a great, nationalistic queen, who defeated the Spanish Armada. Queen Elizabeth II is the present queen who became queen after World War II.

Lesson 3

All of above is true, but if England would have been firmer they could have stopped World War II rather than merely delay it.

Lesson 4

Answers will vary, but it is unlikely. By 1941 England was on her knees and hardly able to win a long, protracted war.

Chapter 34

Lesson 1

The first of these trends was the division of the continent into two antagonistic political, socio-economic, and military blocs, each tied to the power that had liberated it from German occupation. The second was the beginning of the decline of the overseas colonial empires of the major European powers, notably those of Great Britain and France. Everything seemed to point to the relative decline of Europe as a force in the world, as the United States and the Soviet Union assumed the status of the world's sole superpowers in a new bipolar international order. As one historian explained, "The third trend was not nearly as visible as the first two at the end of the war. But it would gradually emerge as a potential antidote to the disease that had afflicted what one observer, applying to postwar Europe a popular reference to the decaying Ottoman Empire before the Great War, called 'the sick man of the world'. This was the movement launched by a small but energetic band of visionaries in favor of the economic and political unity of Europe."

Lesson 2

Soviet ambitions combined with a chauvinistic ideology (i.e., communism) assured that there would be a struggle with England. England, too, with a fear of communism, was more than ready to respond. Ultimately, the Soviet economy was unable to sustain the economic pressures of a 3-decade arms race with England, and its powerful ally America.

Lesson 3

By the end of the decade, things were not going well. Staying in the Middle East had led step-by-step to the confrontation with President Gamal Abdel Nasser in Egypt, and the disastrous decision to seek his overthrow by force in collusion with Israel. The 1956 Suez Crisis was a savage revelation of Britain's financial and military weakness and destroyed much of what remained of Britain's influence in the Middle East. In the colonial territories, more active interference in social and economic matters, with a view to speeding the pace of development, had aroused wide opposition and strengthened nationalist movements. It was becoming much harder for Britain to control the rate of political change, especially where the presence of settlers (as in Kenya and the Rhodesias) sharpened conflicts over land. Britain's position as the third great power and deputy leader of the Western Alliance was threatened by the resurgence of France and West Germany, who jointly presided over the new European Economic Community (EEC). Britain's claim on American support, the indispensable prop of imperial survival, could no longer be taken for granted. And Britain's own economy, far from accelerating, was stuck in a rut.

Lesson 4

Answers will vary.

Chapter 1

A: England has a mild, temperate climate. It is close enough to the European mainland to be easily conquered but far enough away to develop a unique culture. The Britons, and other people groups, never formed a federal government—like the Romans—so they were easily divided and conquered.

B. Druidic practices worked themselves into the Christian Church and remained part of English folklore and superstition for centuries. English institutions, for instance, were always connected to religion. This was a druidic tendency. What societal tendencies? Some scholars argue that British society developed with a strong tertiary tendency (i.e., a respect for authority). At the same time, others argue that druidic influence invited a spirit of individualism and individual rights that likewise emerged in English culture (e.g., Magna Carta).

C. Some scholars argue that this tendency—religion emerging after technology—is the root of the English Industrial Revolution. Technology, then, in Great Britain, always took precedence over religion. Why? No one knows for sure, but many historians argue that technology preceded religion because Britons, Celts, et al., were so keen to develop new weaponry and natural resources (e.g., iron ore) were so abundantly available, that technology developed first. The British were religious of course—witness the druidic influence—but, in general, British leadership never allowed religion to limit technology.

Chapter 2

A. Chesterton's point is that Rome, once weak only on the fringes (e.g., Gaul, Great Britain, Palestine) now was weak everywhere. The collapse of the Roman Empire was not precipitated by outside attacks and influence; it was a failure of Rome itself to adjust to changing times. "The centre had been growing fainter and fainter, and now the centre disappeared. Rome had as much freed the world as ruled it, and now she could rule no more . . . there was anarchy but no rebellion." Furthermore, Chesterton, in the late 19th century, observed that Roman influenced remained—in law, in architecture, in transportation. "It remains to this hour."

B. While the Romans could be and were at times harsh rulers, they were nothing compared to the Anglo-Saxons. The Romans occupied and governed England; the cruel Anglo-Saxons sought to settle, to colonize

Great Britain. The Romans brought culture, order, and peace; the Anglo-Saxons, at least initially, brought havoc and destruction.

Chapter 3

A. Surely the lives of all Americans have been profoundly changed by rapid transportation, television, the Internet, and advances in medicine.

B. Syncretism is perhaps the greatest threat to faith. A biblical example is King Ahab. King Ahab did "more evil than all the kings before him." Ahab, and his wife Jezebel, were good Jews. But they were also good pagans. They tried to keep a foot in both camps—worship of God and worship of Baal. The followers of God found their champion in Elijah, whose history reflects the prophetic teaching of more than one age. His denunciation of syncretism, and his emphatic insistence on the worship of God and Him alone, illustrated by the contest between God and Baal on Mount Carmel, as told in 1 Kings 18, form the key note to a period which culminated in the accession of Jehu, an event in which Elijah's chosen disciple Elisha was the leading figure. King Ahab and Jezebel are very capable, and in many ways, successful monarchs. From their perspective, they are the politically appointed leadership team for Israel. Elijah, and the prophets, were radical, unreasonable, uncompromising troublers of Israel. They were not team players. No doubt Ahab and Jezebel could not understand why Elijah could not carry on a civil discussion about what they saw as tangential, civil issues.

Chapter 4

A. The Magna Carta, or Great Charter concerned the enforcement of certain liberties for the common people and limitations for governments that later influenced other constitutional documents, including the U.S. Constitution.

B. King Herod Antipas was a converted Jew who ruled Palestine under the auspices of the Roman Empire. Two of Herod's sons were Herod Philip and Herod Antipas. Herod Philip married a woman called Herodias. When Herod Antipas visited his brother, he wanted Herodias for a wife for himself. So Herod Antipas divorced his own wife, and married Herodias. She, of course, had to divorce Herod Philip first. The Jewish law does not permit such behavior (Leviticus 18:16 and 20:21). John the Baptist said this was wrong. When he did this, he made

Herodias very angry. So Herod Antipas ordered John's arrest. On one occasion when the king had a party, Herodias' daughter danced for his guests. The king was very pleased with her. He foolishly promised to give her anything that she asked for. The girl asked her mother what to say to the king. Her mother told her to ask Herod to kill John the Baptist. The king did not know what to do. So he beheaded John the Baptist. Herod did not want to do this and in fact Herod thought well of John. Mark 6:20 says that Herod liked to listen to John!

Chapter 5

A. Romans 13 commands believers to obey civil authorities; however, when that civil authority disobeys God, then the believer must disobey civil authority (e.g., Daniel). The believer should do so deferentially, humbly, and publicly, being willing to accept the consequences of his actions.

B. To suggest such a theory is to suggest that Protestantism is a sociological or psychological movement and not a move of the Holy Spirit (which it is). Science and magic had nothing to do with the decision of Martin Luther to embrace a theology that emphasized grace as a prerequisite for salvation. Magic and science had nothing to do with John Knox's high view of Scripture.

Chapter 6

A. Answers will vary, but this author believes that Chesterton was implying that, while Elizabeth I had won many victories, she realized, too, the great events coming in world history. Exploration had begun in earnest. The Industrial Revolution was two centuries away, but already British cottage industries were creating the future. The British political system was the best in the world.

B. Given the chicanery in Elizabethan Protestant England and the pious behavior of King Philip of Spain, one would be hard pressed to say that the defeat of the Armada was the judgment of God on Roman Catholic Spain. Besides, arguably, the "Protestantism" of England was nothing more than Catholicism with the King as the Pope. The Church of England was more Catholic than Protestant.

Chapter 7

This author's respect and admiration for G. K. Chesterton

is second to none but he disagrees with Chesterton. Elizabeth was a transitional monarch, from medieval society to renaissance society. At the same time, "glories did not end with it." Anglican Chesterton might not be thrilled with the advent of a Cromwell, but the Reformed author most certainly sees the emergence of Puritan England as an absolute good thing for England and humanity. Certainly if "its tempestuous torch was soon to be trodden out by the Puritans" a new light the likes of which never seen by mankind was to be lit again. John Milton, William Bradford, Cotton Mather, and John Bunyan all lit a fire that blazed brightly for a generation.

Chapter 8

A. There was a paucity of doctors, and other professionals. Social services suffered. There were labor shortages. In general, Elizabethan society was under great stress.

B. Elizabeth had the means and the will to do so. Besides, it made economic sense. Working Englishmen contributed to society; unemployed, destitute Englishman did not. Queen Elizabeth knew this.

Chapter 9

Answers will vary. In defense of close-minded Christians, one hardly wants to have a faith that has no confessions, no biblical basis. To say all theology is equal is short-sighted. Still, one must be generous in one's acceptance of extraneous matters, as long as the basics are embraced. Having said that, 17th-century Christians had no intention of being tolerant of other faiths. The Pilgrims and Puritans came to America to enjoy freedom of their religion, but they never intended for their citizens to have freedom to follow any other religion!

Chapter 10

A. Clearly Mr. Borglum did not know Edward Taylor or Anne Bradstreet, who were alive, vital people, who loved and lived life with passion. Mr. Borglum is floundering in his stereotypical view of Puritanism. But he has not read the Puritans.

B. They loved God and His Church with an abiding passion.

C. This author prefers Fraser's views. If ever there was a man who was created by circumstances, rather than vice versa, it was Cromwell.

Chapter 11

A. "New" revelation should continually be compared to the inerrant, inspired Word of God. God would not give revelation that violated His unchanging, inviolate, Word.

B. Reinhold Niebuhr, in his book *Moral Man and Immoral Society*, cautions his readers about embracing "herd mentalities." According to him, individuals are morally capable of considering the interests of others and acting. That is, individuals can be unselfish and Godly. Societies, however, find it virtually impossible to handle rationally the competing interests of subgroups. According to Niebuhr, this collective selfishness of individuals-in-groups is overridingly powerful. "In every human group there is less reason to guide and to check impulse, less capacity for self-transcendence, less ability to comprehend the needs of others, therefore more unrestrained egoism than the individuals, who compose the group, reveal in their personal relationships." Politicians—even born-again Christian politicians—may be sincere in their understanding about several issues. In fact, they may be right about some issues. But when that group gains political hegemony, it can lose focus and direction and inadvertently act in an immoral fashion. One final point: societies can force certain behaviors, but it cannot change even one heart. Only God can do that.

C. While one can understand why Cromwell executed Charles I, he turned a recalcitrant, rascally king into a martyr. This was a fatal mistake for the Commonwealth and ultimately precipitated its demise and the restoration of the monarch (i. e., Charles II).

Chapter 12

A. Answers will surely vary. Inevitably in this fallen world, sin will bring judgment on the deserving and on the innocent alike. Without God's mercy all are deserving of His wrath against sin.

B. Charles II expected the English to turn their back on Puritanism altogether and to embrace his so-called "freedom of religion" and thereby advance his Roman Catholic agenda. Such hypocrisy was not effective in the long run.

C. The independent Celtic spirit, and rough handling by the British, assured that Ireland would never be a part of a greater United Kingdom, like Scotland and Wales.

Chapter 13

It is unfortunate that there was so much anti-Catholicism in 17th-century England. But, remember, that only a few years before bloody Queen Mary had executed many Protestants. Still, that does not justify two centuries of prejudice!

Chapter 14

A. This reader respects Chesterton but I feel that he is too hard on poor homesick King George. Chesterton describes the chaos and mediocrity that enveloped the British monarchy for 100 years. To Chesterton two key events are central to the 17th century: the reign of William and Mary and the reign of the Hanovers. The former assumed power peacefully and the later brought an international flavor to the throne whose cosmopolitanism balanced the parochialism of the Oranges.

B. The reign of Queen Anne, which covers the period between William and Mary and George, both foreign monarchs, is the bridge between the time when the aristocrats were at least weak enough to call in a strong man to help them, and the time when they were strong enough deliberately to call in a weak man who would allow them to help themselves. The story of Churchill is primarily the story of the Revolution and how it succeeded; the story of Bolingbroke is the story of the counter-revolution and how it failed. This reader agrees.

Chapter 15

A. Both and neither. King George was no "royal brute" except to the Americans. Actually it was Parliament who controlled the fiscal policy of England, not the King. Likewise, Washington, a somewhat latecomer to the patriot stage, was a reluctant and thoughtful patriot who more than once urged sobriety and caution in the pursuit of liberty.

B. In these postmodern (post–1990 subjectivity and self-centerness) times, Americans could care less about morality in their leaders—as long as these leaders provide the things that these Americans want.

Chapter 16

A. The English had the strongest navy and a capable army. The English economy could more easily sustain a long conflict when other nations could not. These wars were 10–15 years long. This was too difficult for many nations to endure.

B. Answers will vary, however, the Irish always felt closer, ironically, to their oppressive rulers, than foreign powers and have offered troops for every major English war since this time.

Chapter 17

A. Mercantilism is an economic theory that argues that the prosperity of a nation is dependent upon its supply of capital, and that the global volume of international trade is "unchangeable." Economic assets are best increased through a positive balance of trade with other nations (exports minus imports). Mercantilism and Chartered Monopoly Companies were successful British models employed to expand the Empire. The king or queen would give permission, or a chartered monopoly, to explorers to claim lands on his behalf and then authorize certain companies to exploit the natural resources in that part of the world in return for a fixed income to the Monarch. In many ways it was something for nothing for the ruler. These companies would buy the privilege to have a monopoly. For instance, the East India Trading Company had a monopoly on tea trade from India. Besides paying the monarchy a yearly retainer, the East India Company promised to keep prices reasonable. The Spanish and Portuguese used this first, and the French and Dutch followed suit. So, mercantilism worked!

B. The East India Company maintained a predictable monopoly and England obtained tax revenue.

C. The Americans certainly felt justified in their revolution; in retrospect, however, it seems likely that they could have accomplished all their goals without a revolution, if they could have been more patient. Certainly Australia and other Commonwealth countries were able to do so.

Chapter 18

A. Answers will vary. This reader observed how September 11, 2001, no longer has the "sting" it once did. Some misguided Americans recently blamed America for the attack, for instance! Revisionist history will inevitable offer an alternative view of any historical event.

B. The American Revolution produced a new nation, under God, with liberty and justice for all. In comparison to the French Revolution, the American Revolution was practically bloodless. The French Revolution, full of hope and glory, undergirded with giants of philosophy Rousseau and Voltaire, ultimately lead not to liberty and equality, but to a dictator. Some historians explain that this happened because the American nation was founded on the principles of Scripture; the new French Republic was based on base reasoning.

Chapter 19

Philosopher	Religion	Government	Revolution	Violence
William Godwin	Religion to Godwin was a petty, unnecessary, subjective reality that best should be avoided.	Godwin preferred a government that governed the very least.	Revolution was necessary as long as it advanced Godwin's notions of liberality.	Unfortunate, but acceptable if it advanced laudable goals.
Jean-Jacques Rousseau	Opiate of the masses! Mostly bankrupt, manipulative, and counter-revolutionary, the Church was the enemy of the people.	The government that ruled the least was the best.	Revolution was necessary as long as it advanced Rousseau's notions of liberality	Unfortunate, but acceptable if it advanced laudable goals.
Thomas Paine	Paine was a cynic and an agnostic. Religion was useful only so long as it advanced this humanist agenda.	The government that ruled the least was the best.	Revolution was desirable.	Unavoidable and regrettable, but necessary.
Edmund Burke	Very important and necessary to a free, productive society.	Government was necessary, and laudable, as long as it was a representative democracy that balanced the needs of the society at large with the needs of the individual.	Revolution was virtually never necessary.	Violence was at times necessary.

Chapter 20

All of the above is true but he might add that the Napoleonic Wars killed 1 million French soldiers, 1.5 million allied soldiers, and 3.5 million civilians. France had been at war almost incessantly for over 20 years. She had lost millions of men and her colonies, her overseas trade was strangled, and she was virtually bankrupt. The French, their country defeated and occupied, also lost any hope of national reconciliation.

Chapter 21

I would do my best to employ as many workers as I could from my older plant. Those I could not hire I would retire if possible with a decent pension and others I would compensate with a generous unemployment allowance for up to 2 years.

Chapter 22

A. By this time, religion was under attack from Darwinism and other naturalistic world views. Furthermore, the family was in decline, partly because of the Industrial Revolution.

B. The contents of the toilets were deposited in the Thames and other rivers in Great Britain.

C. In spite of great prosperity, many workers could not afford the inflated prices. British society was polarized more and more.

Chapter 23

This reader respectfully disagrees with Mr. Thompson. The Victorian Era was a long period of prosperity for the British people, as profits gained from the overseas British Empire, as well as from industrial improvements at home, allowed an educated middle class to develop. It was a time, too, of moral stability and decency that has rarely been exhibited by a civilization in all of world history.

Chapter 24

A. Little did Carlyle know! The Victorians, indeed, as generations before them, questioned the efficacy of the Word of God in its application to human life. This will continue forever.

B. Clearly *Punch* magazine did not know Booth at all. Booth was one of the most humble, unselfish men in Victorian England who only wanted to relieve misery and poverty. Most of all though, he wanted to "blow God's trumpet" and to bring glory to God in every way.

Chapter 25

A. American policy makers understand the problem with nation building in a nation as diverse as Afghanistan. They wish only to protect American interests by encouraging a strong emerging democratic Afghan government that will presumably limit Al-Qaida activity in this volatile region.

B. Primarily the geography of the region makes it difficult. Also divergent religious groups and ethnic groups exacerbate this difficult situation.

Chapter 26

A. Al-Mahdi is "the rightly-guided one" who, according to Islamic traditions will come before the end of time to make the entire world Muslim. Over the last fourteen hundred years numerous claimants to the mantle of the Mahdi have arisen in both Shi`i and Sunni circles. Modern belief in the coming of the Mahdi has manifested most famously in the 1979 uprising of Saudi Arabia, and most recently in the ongoing Mahdist movements (some violent) in Iraq, as well as in the frequently expressed public prayers of Iranian President Ahmadinejad bidding the Mahdi to return and, in the larger Sunni Islamic world, by claims that the late Osama bin Ladin might be the Mahdi. The President would be wise to act forcefully and quickly to thwart the efforts of this aberrant, violent movement.

B. Answers will vary. At this time the British government had many ancilliary reasons to stay: loyal indigent followers, British citizens, and commercial interests.

Chapter 27

The British Empire brought advances in culture in all people groups it touched. It brought relative peace and prosperity to millions of people.

Chapter 28

Modern art refers to artistic works produced during the period extending roughly from 1870 to the 1990s. This art form casts to the side traditions of the past have been thrown aside in a spirit of experimentation. A tendency toward abstraction is characteristic of much modern art. Thus, "love" is presented through a word sculpture rather than a mother holding a child or two couples embracing. This is a modernist way to capture in a new, innovative way, an old subject.

Chapter 29

A. In spite of the family relationships, their national identity was stronger.

B. Consider the following essay by historian Suzanne Karpilovsky:

World War I was the result of leaders' aggression towards other countries which was supported by the rising nationalism of the European nations. Economic and imperial competition and fear of war prompted military alliances and an arms race, which further escalated the tension contributing to the outbreak of war. At the settlement of the Congress of Vienna in 1815, the principle of nationalism was ignored in favor of preserving the peace. Germany and Italy were left as divided states, but strong nationalist movements and revolutions led to the unification of Italy in 1861 and that of Germany in 1871. Another result of the Franco-Prussian War of 1870-71 was that France was left seething over the loss of Alsace-Lorraine to Germany, and Revanche was a major goal of the French. Nationalism posed a problem for Austria-Hungary and the Balkans, areas comprised of many conflicting national groups. The ardent Panslavism of Serbia and Russia's willingness to support its Slavic brother conflicted with Austria-Hungary's Pan-Germanism .Another factor which contributed to the increase in rivalry in Europe was imperialism. Great Britain, Germany and France needed foreign markets after the increase in manufacturing caused by the Industrial Revolution. These countries competed for economic expansion in Africa.

Although Britain and France resolved their differences in Africa, several crises foreshadowing the war involved the clash of Germany against Britain and France in North Africa. In the Middle East, the crumbling Ottoman Empire was alluring to Austria-Hungary, the Balkans and Russia. World War I was caused in part by the two opposing alliances developed by Bismarckian diplomacy after the Franco-Prussian War. In order to diplomatically isolate France, Bismarck formed the Three Emperor's League in 1872, an alliance between Germany, Russia and Austria-Hungary. When the French occupied Tunisia, Bismarck took advantage of Italian resentment towards France and created the Triple Alliance between Germany, Italy and Austria-Hungary in 1882. In exchange for Italy's agreement to stay neutral if war broke out between Austria-Hungary and Russia, Germany and Austria-Hungary would protect Italy from France. Russia and Austria-Hungary grew suspicious of each other over conflicts in the Balkans in 1887, but Bismarck repaired the damage to his alliances with a Reinsurance Treaty with Russia, allowing both powers to stay neutral if the other was at war. However, after Bismarck was fired by Kaiser William II in 1890, the traditional dislike of Slavs kept Bismarck's successors from renewing the understanding with Russia. France took advantage of this opportunity to get an ally, and the Franco-Russian Entente was formed in 1891, which became a formal alliance in 1894. The Kruger telegram William II sent to congratulate the leader of the Boers for defeating the British in 1896, his instructions to the German soldiers to behave like Huns in China during the Boxer Rebellion, and particularly the large-scale navy he was building all contributed to British distrust of Germany. As a result, Britain and France overlooked all major imperialistic conflict between them and formed the Entente Cordiale in 1904.

Russia formed an Entente with Britain in 1907 after they had reached an understanding with Britain's ally Japan and William II had further alienated Russia by supporting Austrian ambitions in the Balkans. The Triple Entente, an informal coalition between Great Britain, France and Russia, now countered the Triple Alliance. International tension was greatly increased by the division of Europe into two armed camps. The menace of the hostile division led to an arms race, another cause of World War I. Acknowledging that Germany was the leader in military organization and efficiency, the great powers of Europe copied the universal conscription, large reserves and detailed planning of the Prussian system. Technological and organizational developments led to the formation of general staffs with precise plans for mobilization and attack that often could not be reversed once they were begun. The German von Schlieffen Plan to attack France before Russia in the event of war with Russia was one such complicated plan that drew more countries into war than necessary. Armies and navies were greatly expanded. The standing armies of France and Germany doubled in size between 1870 and 1914. Naval expansion was also extremely competitive, particularly between Germany and Great Britain.

By 1889, the British had established the principle that in order to maintain naval superiority in the event of war they would have to have a navy two and a half times as large as the second-largest navy. This motivated the British to launch the Dreadnought, invented by Admiral Sir John Fisher, in 1906. The Russo-Japanese War of 1904-1905 had demonstrated how effective these battleships were. As Britain increased their output of battleships, Germany correspondingly stepped up their naval production,

including the Dreadnought. Although efforts for worldwide disarmament were made at the Hague Conferences of 1899 and 1907, international rivalry caused the arms race to continue to feed on itself. The friction of an armed and divided Europe escalated into several crises in Morocco and the Balkans which nearly ended in war. In 1905, Germany announced its support of independence for Morocco, the African colony which Britain had given France in 1904. The British defended the French, and war was avoided by a international conference in Algeciras in 1906 which allowed France to make Morocco a French protectorate. Another conflict was incited by the Austria-Hungarian annexation of the former Turkish province of Bosnia in 1908. The Greater Serbian movement had as an object the acquisition of Slavic Bosnia, so Serbia threatened war on Austria-Hungary. Russia had pledged their support to Serbia, so they began to mobilize, which caused Germany, allied with Austria-Hungary, to threaten war on Russia.

The beginning of World War I was postponed when Russia backed down, but relations between Austria-Hungary and Serbia were greatly strained. A second Moroccan crisis occurred in 1911 when Germany sent a warship to Agadir in protest of French supremacy in Morocco, claiming the French had violated the agreement at Algeciras. Britain again rose to France's defense and gave the Germans stern warnings. Germany agreed to allow France a free hand in Morocco in exchange for part of the French Congo. In the Balkan Wars of 1912-13, the Balkan States drove the Turks back to Constantinople and fought among themselves over territory. Tensions between Serbia and Austria-Hungary increased when Austria-Hungary forced Serbia to abandon some of its gains. Europe had reached its breaking point when on June 28, 1914, Archduke Francis Ferdinand, heir to the Austria-Hungarian throne, was assassinated in Sarajevo, Bosnia, by a Serbian nationalist belonging to an organization known as the Black Hand (Narodna Obrana). Immediately following the assassination Germany pledged its full support (blank check) to Austria-Hungary, pressuring them to declare war on Serbia, while France strengthened its backing of Russia. Convinced that the Serbian government had conspired against them, Austria-Hungary issued Serbia an unacceptable ultimatum, to which Serbia consented almost entirely.

Unsatisfied, Austria-Hungary declared war on Serbia on July 28, 1914. On July 29, Russia ordered a partial mobilization only against Austria-Hungary in support of Serbia, which escalated into a general mobilization. The Germans threatened war on July 31 if the Russians did not demobilize. Upon being asked by Germany what it would do in the event of a Russo-German War, France responded that it would act in its own interests and mobilized. On August 1, Germany declared war on Russia, and two days later, on France. The German invasion of Belgium to attack France, which violated Belgium's official neutrality, prompted Britain to declare war on Germany. World War I had begun.

Chapter 30

Civilization had never known anything like World War I. It was horrible beyond one's wildest imagination. No war had come remotely close. It was not just the substantial casualties. It was also the invention of the machine gun, the tank, and poison gas. Trench warfare. Airplane bombing. These were all part of World War I.

Chapter 31

I would have recognized that there were no victims, only perpetrators. I would create something like the Marshal Plan (after World War II the Marshal plan rebuilt Europe) to rebuild all of Europe. The Marshall Plan provided low-interest loans and grants to devastated European areas that created goodwill and strong economies in a relatively short amount of time. I would remove the war guilt clause and reparations. Europe should remain essentially the same way it did before 1914 (except for the creation of ethnic countries like Serbia).

Chapter 32

As late as 1936 it was within England's power to stop these three rogue countries from developing their armies and waging war. England had the resources, the man-power, and most of all, the navy to enforce its will on these nations. If England would have, for instance, objected to Germany's annexation of the Rhineland, the Germans would have backed down. If England would have fought Italy in Africa in the 1930s she would not have had to fight her in 1940. Finally, if England had cornered Japan after Japan attacked China, Japan no doubt would have backed down.

Chapter 33

5   D-Day

3   The London Blitz

1   The Munich Conference

4   Pearl Harbor

2   Winston Churchill is elected prime minister

Germany was never able to defeat the Royal Navy and therefore a safe crossing of the English channel was impossible. By the summer of 1941, also, Hitler was planning to invade the Soviet Union. Hitler was sure that he could invade and conquer Russia and then turn and conquer England at his leisure. Besides, Hitler was an Anglophile and hoped that England would join his army in its struggle against Communist Soviet Union.

Chapter 34

Answers will vary.

Write
Articulately.

Think
Critically.

Live
Biblically.

Integrate 3 Years of
High School Literature
with History

2 Hours a Day
Yields 3
Course Credits
a Year

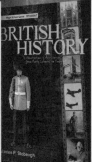

Master Books®
A Division of New Leaf Publishing Group
www.masterbooks.net

Teacher | 978-0-89051-672-0   Teacher | 978-0-89051-674-4   Teacher | 978-0-89051-676-8   Teacher | 978-0-89051-643-0   Teacher | 978-0-89051-645-4   Teacher | 978-0-89051-647-8
Student | 978-0-89051-671-3   Student | 978-0-89051-673-7   Student | 978-0-89051-675-1   Student | 978-0-89051-644-7   Student | 978-0-89051-646-1   Student | 978-0-89051-648-5

Coursework developed by Dr. James Stobaugh:
Ordained pastor, certified secondary teacher, SAT coach, recognized homeschool leader, and author

4,000 Fossil Whales

Concerned abou
SCIENCE
and a BIBLICA
worldview?

100,000 Fossil Turtle Specimens

500,000 Fossil Fish

75,000 Horse Skeletons or Skeleton Fragments

**NATURAL SCIENC
THE STORY OF ORIG**

Parent Lesson Plan
(PLP)

EVOLUTI
THE GRAND EXPE
*The Quest for
an Answer*

EVOLUTION:
THE GRAND EXPERIMENT VOL. 1
— Dr. Carl Werner —

TEACHER'S M

EVOLUTION:
THE GRAND EXPERIMENT

**1-year course
10th-12th grade
½ credit**

3 Book,
1 DVD Package
$71.99 Retail

Natural Science
The Story of Origins
NEW Curriculum from Master Books

All photos from the book!

Enjoy a truly unique science exploration that presents a detailed discussion of evolution and creation, allowing students to discover for themselves the answers to common questions about the Biblical account of creation and how it fits into the fossil record.

100,000 Fossil Dinosaurs

Nearly 1,000 Fossil Flying Reptiles

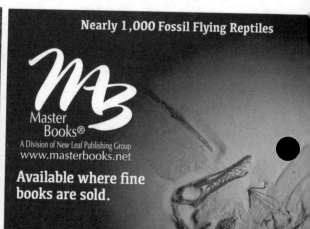

Master Books®
A Division of New Leaf Publishing Group
www.masterbooks.net

**Available where fine
books are sold.**